Karl Friedrich Schinkel
Charlottenhof, Potsdam-Sanssouci

Text
Heinz Schönemann

Photographien/Photographs
Reinhard Görner

Edition Axel Menges

Herausgeber/Editor: Axel Menges

© 2012 Edition Axel Menges, Stuttgart/London
ISBN 978-3-930698-12-7

Zweite, überarbeitete Auflage/Second, improved
edition

Reproduktionen/Reproductions: Bild und Text GmbH
Baun, Fellbach; Reinhard Görner, Berlin
Druck und Bindearbeiten/Printing and binding:
Graspo CZ, a. s., Zlín, Tschechische Republik/Czech
Republic

Übersetzung ins Englische/Translation into English:
Michael Robinson

Gestaltung/Design: Axel Menges

Inhalt

Contents

Charlottenhof oder Siam – ein preußisches Utopia

Als Peter Joseph Lenné 1816 nach Potsdam berufen wurde, legte er dem König Friedrich Wilhelm III. seinen großen, in wochenlanger Arbeit gezeichneten Plan zur Umwandlung des langgestreckten friderizianischen Sanssouci-Gartens in einen Landschaftspark vor: »Plan von Sans, Souci und dessen Umgebungen, nebst Project fliessendes und springendes Wasser dahinzubringen, so wie auch die Promenaden zu verschönern. Entworfen und gezeichnet von P: J: Lenné. 1816.« Da er auch die Umgebungen des Gartens mit topographischer Genauigkeit festgehalten hatte, erschien am linken unteren Ende des 89 x 193 cm großen Plans, also weit im Südwesten des bearbeiteten Gebietes eine rechteckige Hofanlage. Sie lag westlich des den Parkgraben mit der Havel verbindenden Schafgrabens, nach Norden bis an den trennenden Parkgraben heran waren ihr unregelmäßig geschnittene Acker- und Wiesenflächen zugeordnet. Im Süden erstreckte sich über Lennés Plan hinaus bis an den dort zu denkenden Werderschen Weg ein alleenartig gegliederter Bereich regelmäßiger Nutzgärten und eine dreieckige Gehölzgruppe, an deren östlichem Rand eine Zugangsallee auf die mittlere Weidefläche führte. Unabhängig davon lag weiter westlich in leichter Diagonale zu den Koordinaten des Plans, von umlaufenden Alleen gefaßt und mit Baumreihen in schmale Querflächen geteilt, ein größeres rechteckiges Feld. Es wurde von einem unregelmäßig verlaufenden Entwässerungsgraben berührt, der zusammen mit anderen Gräben das ganze Gelände durchzog, dessen Verbindungen zu Parkgraben und Gracht des Neuen Palais auf Lennés Darstellung jedoch unklar blieben. Bei diesem Anwesen handelt es sich um das damals schon »Charlottenhof« genannte Vorwerk, auf das Lenné kaum ein Jahrzehnt später die Aufmerksamkeit der Krone lenken sollte, und um das nochmals ein Jahrzehnt weiter hinzuerworbene Ackerstück für die Anlage des Hippodroms.

In dieser einsamen Gegend, die als sumpfig und häufig überschwemmt geschildert wurde, hatte der Baumeister des Holländischen Viertels Johann Boumann d. Ä. 1746 ein Grundstück erworben und darauf Scheune und Stall, später ein Wohnhaus errichtet und einen Garten angelegt. Er verkaufte es aber schon 1755 an den Windmüller Kaene, von dem es 1757 Landbaumeister Johann Büring übernahm und in der Folge beträchtlich erweiterte. Danach erscheint das Anwesen als »Büringsches Vorwerk« in den Stadtkarten von Potsdam. 1770 ersteigerte Carl von Gontard das Gehöft, aber auch er besaß es nur ein Jahrzehnt, von ihm kaufte der Erbpächter des Kammervorwerks Johann Christian Hoff 1780 erst Äcker und Nebengebäude, dann 1783 auch Wohnhaus und Garten. Über den Koch Martin Friedrich Weber kam mit Kaufvertrag vom 8. Mai 1794 »... das Gut ehedem Bürings Meyerey, jetzt Charlottenhof genannt« an die Witwe Maria Charlotte von Genzkow. Damit waren die häufigen Wechsel noch nicht zu Ende: 1795 erwarb es der Musiker Dupont, von ihm 1796 Heinrich Werner von Tresckow, dann 1798 Domänenrat Claussen und 1800 der Johanniter-Malteser-Ritter von Alvensleben. Drei Jahre später besaß es Kaufmann Holtze, der zwar 1822 noch umfangreiche Instandsetzungen vornahm, es aber 1825 wiederum zum Verkauf stellte.

Für Lenné bot sich nun die Gelegenheit, eine Ausdehnung des Parkes Sanssouci nach Südwesten zu betreiben. Kronprinz Friedrich Wilhelm (IV.) war von diesen Plänen ebenso eingenommen wie von der Idee eines an diesem Ort gemeinsam mit Karl Friedrich Schinkel zu realisierenden Vorhabens.

Schinkel und Lenné sind zuerst auf den Besitzungen des Fürsten Hardenberg zu gemeinsamer Arbeit zusammengekommen. Es ergab sich eine einmalige Partnerschaft, die nur mit den glanzvollen Jahren des Zusammenwirkens von Humphry Repton und John Nash verglichen werden kann.

Lenné hatte im Juli 1815 Schönbrunn und Laxenburg verlassen und sich in die Unsicherheit einer freien Betätigung in seine nunmehr preußische Heimat zurückbegeben. Der gesicherten Position in Laxenburg zog er eine Anstellung »als Gartengehilfe auf Probe« beim Hofgärtner des Neuen Gartens in Potsdam vor, obwohl er vorerst nur beauftragt war, von den königlichen Gärten Aufnahmen und Zeichnungen anzufertigen. Hinter seiner weiteren Entwicklung ist der Einfluß des Staatskanzlers Carl August von Hardenberg zu vermuten, für den Lenné als seine erste Arbeit den Entwurf des Gartenraums zwischen Schloß Glienicke und dem Jungfernsee übernahm und im Herbst desselben Jahres ausführte.

Hardenberg hatte Preußen gemeinsam mit Wilhelm von Humboldt auf dem Wiener Kongreß vertreten und muß wohl schon dort in nähere Beziehung zu Lenné gekommen sein. Wenn Hardenberg in seinen Staatstheorien das Gemeinwesen mit einem Baum verglich, ist es wohl nicht abwegig, bei ihm und Humboldt weitreichende Pläne der Landesgestaltung durch den Einsatz Schinkels und die Anwerbung Lennés vorauszusetzen. Schinkel war bereits seit 1814 in Glienicke tätig; sein Arbeitsfeld erweiterte sich auf die umfassende Erneuerung des Schlosses, nachdem Hardenberg den Besitz erworben hatte. Wilhelm von Humboldt, der Schinkel schon aus seiner römischen Zeit kannte, hatte ihn 1810 der Königin Luise vorgestellt und ihm bei der Oberbaudeputation eine Anstellung als geheimer Bauassessor verschafft, die er am 10. Mai 1810 antrat. Anschauliches Ergebnis der Gemeinsamkeit von Schinkel und Lenné ist die nach dem Übergang von Glienicke an den Prinzen Karl 1824 unternommene Umgestaltung des Billardhauses und seiner Umgebung auf dem hohen Ufer über dem Jungfernsee zum Kasino.

Beide gaben sich dabei als von Durand beeinflußt zu erkennen und bestätigten sich gegenseitig in ihrer Prägung durch dessen normative Lehre. Schinkel hatte vor seiner ersten, 1803 angetretenen Italienreise die für ihn erreichbaren Publikationen Durands zur Kenntnis genommen und sich in seinen Reisezielen von ihnen beeinflussen lassen. Lenné hatte während seines Studienaufenthaltes in Paris 1811/12 auch den Architekturkurs von Durand besucht. Daher war ihnen beiden Durands Hauptwerk (Jean-Nicholas-Louis Durand, *Recueil et parallèle des édifices de tout genre, anciens et modernes*, Paris 1800), genannt »Le Grand Durand«, bekannt. Dessen Titelseite ist von einer Vignettenleiste gerahmt, auf der sich nicht nur ein »Vestibule d'une Maison à Rome« findet, das für Schinkels Charlottenhof Bedeutung erlangen sollte, sondern auch eine »Auberge d'Italie«, in der man bis ins Detail das Vorbild für das Kasino in Glienicke ausmachen kann. Das betrifft weniger das Haus selbst als die Per-

Charlottenhof or Siam – a Prussian utopia

When Peter Joseph Lenné was called to Potsdam in 1816 he presented King Friedrich Wilhelm II a major plan, the product of weeks of work, for transforming the extensive gardens of Sanssouci, which were in the style of Frederick the Great, into a landscaped park: »Plan of Sans, Souci and its environs, along with a project to introduce flowing and leaping water into it, and also for beautifying the promenades. Designed and drawn by P: J: Lenné. 1816.« As he had also recorded the area surrounding the gardens with topographical precision, a rectangular farm plot appeared at the left-hand lower end of the 89 x 193 cm plan, in other words in the far south-west of the area covered. It was west of the Schafgraben, a moat or ditch linking the Parkgraben and the Havel. To the north, right up to the dividing Parkgraben, it included irregular patterns of ploughed fields and meadows. To the south, extending beyond Lenné's plan to the Werderscher Weg, whose position can be imagined, was an area divided as if by avenues of regular kitchen gardens and a triangular patch of timber. On the eastern edge of this, an avenue gave access to the central area of pasture. Independent of this, and further to the west, on a slight diagonal to the coordinates of the plan, framed by avenues running round it and divided into narrow transverse areas by rows of trees, was a large, rectangular field. It was touched by an irregularly disposed drainage ditch, which, along with other ditches, ran through the whole site. However, their connection with the Parkgraben and the ditch at the Neues Palais remained unclear in Lenné's presentation. This estate consisted in fact of the outlying farm already called »Charlottenhof«, to which Lenné was to draw the attention of the crown scarcely a decade later, and also included the piece of arable land later acquired for the Hippodrome a further ten years later.

Johann Boumann the Elder, architect of the Dutch Quarter, had acquired a plot in this lonely area, which was presented as marshy and frequently flooded, in 1746. He built a barn and a stable there, and later a house with its own garden. But he sold it to a windmill owner called Kaene as early as 1755, from whom it was taken over in 1757 by farmer Johan Büring, who subsequently extended it considerably. After this the estate appears as »Büring's farmstead« on the Pots-

dam town maps. In 1770 the farm was bought at auction by Carl von Gontard, but he too owned it for only a decade. The hereditary leaseholder of the demesne, Johann Christian Hoff, first bought the fields and outbuildings in 1780, and then the house and garden in 1783. Then, via the cook Martin Friedrich Werber, »... the estate formerly called Büring's dairy, now Charlottenhof« came to the widow Maria Charlotte von Genzkow as a result of the contract of sale dated 8 May 1794. But even this was not the last of these frequent changes: in 1795 it was acquired by a musician called Dupont, Heinrich Werner von Tresckow acquired it from him in 1796, then demesne councillor Carlsen in 1798 and von Alvensleben, a Knight of St. John of Malta, in 1800. Three years later it was in the hands of a merchant called Holtze, who undertook considerable repairs in 1822, but put it back on the market in 1825.

Lenné was now presented with the opportunity of extending the Sanssouci park to the south-west. Crown Prince Friedrich Wilhelm (IV) was as enthusiastic about these plans as he was about the idea of an architectural project to be realized jointly with Karl Friedrich Schinkel on this site.

Schinkel and Lenné first worked together on Prince Hardenberg's property. This led to a unique partnership comparable only with the magnificent years when Humphry Repton and John Nash worked together.

Lenné had left Schönbrunn and Laxenburg in July 1817 and returned to the uncertainty of free-lance work in what was to be his Prussian home. He preferred a job as »garden assistant on probation« with the court gardener in the Neuer Garten in Potsdam to the secure position in Laxenburg, even though at first his only work was to prepare records and drawings of the royal gardens. Presumably State Chancellor Carl August von Hardenberg was behind his advancement. Lenné took on designing the area of garden between Schloß Glienicke and the Jungfernsee as his first task, and completed the work in autumn of the first year.

Hardenberg had represented Prussia at the Congress of Vienna, with Wilhelm von Humboldt, and must have got to know Lenné well there. When Hardenberg compared the state with a tree in his theory of statecraft, it is probably reasonable to assume that he and Humboldt had far-reaching plans for landscape design in mind, using Schinkel and recruiting Lenné.

1. Peter Joseph Lenné, *Plan von Sans, Souci und dessen Umgebungen nebst Project fliessendes und springendes Wasser dahinzubringen, so wie auch die Promenaden zu verschönern. Entworfen und gezeichnet von P: J: Lenné. 1816*. Feder, laviert. SPSG, Planslg. 3674.

1. Peter Joseph Lenné, *Plan of Sans, Souci and its environs, along with a project to introduce flowing and leaping water into it, and also for beautifying the promenades. Designed and drawn by P: J: Lenné. 1816*. Pen, washed. SPSG, Planslg. 3674.

SPSG: Stiftung Preußische Schlösser und Gärten Berlin-Brandenburg, Potsdam-Sanssouci.
SMPK: Stiftung Preußischer Kulturbesitz, Berlin.

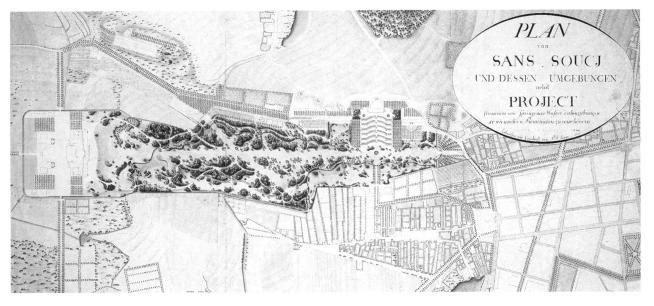

golen und die Terrassenmauer. Schinkel verlängerte den parallel zum Jungfernsee gelagerten Bau mit seitlich angesetzten Pergolen, »Gegenständen der Natur bei der Komposition von Gebäuden«, wie Durand vorgeschlagen hatte, während eine weitere Pergola, dem Gebäude zum abfallenden Ufer vorgelagert, trotz der geringen Höhe des Hanges die Andeutung einer Terrassenanlage wie in italienischen Renaissancegärten entstand, mit der es Lenné gelang, die Urform für die künftig in seinem Werk wichtig werdenden Terrassengärten zu finden.

Schinkel und Lenné hatten es als ersten Schritt ihrer künftigen Zusammenarbeit vollbracht, ein bescheidenes altes Haus in ein Glanzstück neuer Architekturauffassung zu verwandeln. Aus dem alten Billardhaus schufen sie ein Kasino über der Seenlandschaft der Havel, in dem sich wie in einem Focus romantische Lebens- und Weltsicht bündelte. Zwei den Planungen zum Kasino nahestehende Zeichnungen des Kronprinzen lassen dessen Teilnahme am gemeinsamen Tun Schinkels und Lennés erkennen. Von hier dürfte dann auch die durch Lenné betriebene Erwerbung der Gutsanlage Charlottenhof für den Kronprinzen und des Babelsbergs für den Prinzen Wilhelm ihren Ausgang genommen haben. Der gelungene Umbau und die Aufstockung des einfachen Billardhauses zu einem zeitgenössischen Bauwerk werden den Kronprinzen von der Realisierbarkeit seines ähnlichen Vorhabens am Gutshaus Charlottenhof überzeugt haben. Als Lenné auf eine Erweiterung des friderizianischen Gartens durch Erwerb und Umbau von Charlottenhof drängte, fand er deshalb schnell Zustimmung.

Nunmehr forderte König Friedrich Wilhelm III. mit Kabinettsorder vom 7. Dezember 1825 den Hofmarschall von Maltzahn zur gutachtlichen Äußerung auf. Dessen am 20. Dezember unmittelbar an den König gerichteter Bericht ist ohne Zweifel von Lenné zugearbeitet und damit ein erster Beleg für dessen zielstrebiges Vorgehen, aus den verstreuten königlichen und herrschaftlichen Gärten um Potsdam eine große Parklandschaft zu fügen, die von historischen und topographischen Zufällen gesetzte Grenzen überschreitet. »Ew. königlichen Majestät berichte ich ... über die zu machende Acquisition des Gutes Charlottenhof, daß die Vereinigung dieses Grundstückes mit dem Garten von Sanssouci bedeutend zur Verschönerung dieses Gartens beitragen würde. Der Teil des Gartens, worin der Freundschaftstempel liegt, ist sehr schmal. Da dieses Grundstück nun hier anstößt, so würden die neuen Partien desselben mehr Ausdehnung ohne große Kosten bekommen können, wodurch die ganze Anlage aber bedeutend gewinnen würde. Solange das Gut in den Händen des jetzigen Besitzers ungetrennt bleibt, wird es immer ein angenehmes Bild von dem Garten von Sanssouci aus bleiben und die Acquisition nicht nötig sein; da er aber, wie ich höre, verkaufen muß, ... so steht sehr zu befürchten, daß er dasselbe in kleinen Parzellen zu verkaufen suchen würde, da er es auf diese Weise bei der Nähe von Potsdam unstreitig am Höchsten benutzen würde. Der Garten von Sanssouci würde dann aber wahrscheinlich mit Kraut- und Kohlgärten umgeben werden und dadurch dieser Teil des Gartens unendlich verlieren.«

Der König kaufte, der Kronprinz erhielt Weihnachten 1825 das Gelände zum Geschenk, schon mit Lennés Vorplanung, eigenen Vorsätzen und ganz ohne Zweifel Schinkels Umbauauftrag.

Schloß und Park Charlottenhof, vom Kronprinzen »Siam« genannt, unterscheiden sich von den Architekturträumen, Burgen- und Palastvisionen, die Friedrich Wilhelm IV. in allen Lebensaltern bewegten. Die Ritter- und Nixenspiele des Knaben und seiner Geschwister ließen die Felsenburg oder das Inselkloster »St. Georgen im See« aus den Fluten der Havelseen auftauchen; dem Heranwachsenden, der mit seinen Brüdern schwimmend die Potsdamer Havel zwischen Tornow und Hermannswerder überwand, erschien auf dem jenseitigen Ufer ein »Belriguardo« der Sehnsucht als hochgelegenes Schloß; vor dem treuen Leser Fouqués baute sich auf steilem Gebirge »Frau Minnetrosts Warte« in die Höhe; der Kronprinz, der um ein würdiges Denkmal für Friedrich den Großen stritt, entwickelte das monumentale Projekt einer »via triumphalis«, die von Norden her den Garten des großen Vorfahren wie ein Geschichtspanorama umfassen sollte. Die Anlage von Schloß und Park Charlottenhof verfolgte von Anfang an höhere Ziele.

Der Kronprinz zählte Schinkel zu seinen Lehrern, mindestens was die Baukunst und das Zeichnen betraf. Die Unterweisung des Kronprinzen durch Schinkel erfolgte stets an konkreten Beispielen aus dessen Praxis. Den Entstehungsprozeß von Park und Schloß Charlottenhof begleitete er mit einer ungewöhnlich großen Zahl von Skizzen und Entwürfen und schätzte selbst seinen Anteil an der Planung sehr hoch, sprach und schrieb von »Siam« und bezeichnete sich sogar in dieser Zeit scherzhaft als einen Architekten aus Siam. Ein Erinnerungsblatt aus Venedig ist signiert »Architetto – Frederigo Siamese 1829«; auch Grundrißzeichnungen zu Umbauvorschlägen im Berliner Schloß und als Sommernachtsträume bezeichnete Entwürfe für das Stadtpalais des Prinzen Wilhelm tragen solche Unterschriften: »FW Siamhouse architect« oder alle seine Necknamen: »Fritz Siam Butt«.

Diesen Namen »der Butt« hatte Friedrich Wilhelm mit Selbstironie angenommen und die Bezeichnung »Butt« für das eigene Bildnis als Signatur ausgewählter Zeichnungen und als Paraphe unter Briefen und privaten Mitteilungen benutzt. Butt galt als scherzhafte Übernahme des traditionellen Titels für den Thronfolger, wie er sich im französischen »Dauphin« erhalten hat. »Ad usum delphini« waren die Erziehungsprogramme bezeichnet, die, zur Bildung eines künftigen Herrschenden zusammengestellt, das gesamte Wissen einer Zeit enzyklopädisch ordneten und in jugendlich faßliche Form brachten. In Charlottenhof gewinnt der Name symbolhafte Bedeutung. Das Service für den Schloßgebrauch trägt auf allen seinen Teilen den goldenen Butt in leuchtend blauem Fond, umgeben von den Buchstaben »SIAM«; in den Römischen Bädern nimmt der Butt die Gestalt eines großen wasserspeienden Fisches an: der Schloßherr selbst beim Gärtnerhaus als »fons vitae«.

Siam, nach dem Verständnis der Zeit das »Land der Freien«, war durchaus kein ungewöhnlicher Name für ein Arkadien oder Utopia. Schon die Kurfürstin und Königin Sophie Charlotte hatte sich für das ferne Land interessiert und ihre Lektüre der Reisebriefe von Simon de la Loubère (*Du Royaume de Siam*, Amsterdam 1691) mit Leibniz diskutiert. Dem Großen Kurfürsten lag die Exotik der holländischen Gebiete in Südamerika und China als Alternativmodell zu Europa näher. China und die China-Mode veranlaßte noch Friedrich den Großen zum Bau eines Gartenpavillons, während

Schinkel had been working in Glienicke since 1814; his work expanded to include comprehensive renovation of the palace after Hardenberg had acquired it. Wilhelm von Humboldt, whom Schinkel knew from his period in Rome, had introduced him to Queen Luise in 1810 and secured him employment as privy assessor of buildings to the building commission, with which he started work on 10 May 1810. One striking result of the joint presence of Schinkel and Lenné was seen in Glienicke after Prince Karl took it over in 1824 where they converted the billiard house and its surroundings on the high bank above the Jungfernsee into a casino.

Both men showed how they had been influenced by Durand and his normative teaching in this project. Schinkel had taken note of Durand's publication that were available to him before his first visit to Italy in 1803, and was influenced by him in his choice of destination. Lenné had attended Durand's architecture course while studying in Paris in 1811/12. They were thus both familiar with Durand's major work, called »Le Grand Durand« (Jean-Nicholas-Louis Durand, *Recueil et parallèle des édifices de tout genre, anciens et modernes*, Paris 1800). Its title page is framed by a strip of vignettes in which there is not only a »Vestibule d'une Maison à Rome« that was to be important for Schinkel's Charlottenhof, but also an »Auberge d'Italie« that can be seen as a model for the Glienicke casino, down to the last detail. This applies less to the building itself than to the pergolas and the terrace wall. Schinkel extended the building, which runs parallel to the Jungfernsee, with pergolas placed at the sides, »objects of nature in the composition of buildings«, as Durand had suggested, while another pergola, placed in front of the building on the sloping bank side, which produced a hint of a terrace of the kind found in Italian Renaissance gardens, despite the fact that the slope was not very great. Here Lenné successfully found the essential form for the terrace gardens that were to be so important in his future work.

Schinkel and Lenné had made the first step in their future cooperation by transforming a modest old building into a brilliant specimen of a new kind of architecture. They made the old billiards house into a casino set above the lake landscape which concentrated a Romantic view of life and the world in precise focus. Two drawings by the Crown Prince that were close to Schinkel's and Lenné's plans show how he was involved in their joint activities. This have been why the Charlottenhof farmland was acquired for the Crown Prince and Babelsberg for Prince Wilhelm, both under the influence of Lenné. The successful conversion and addition of a storey to the simple billiards building to make it into a piece of contemporary architecture will have convinced the Crown Prince that his similar project for the Charlottenhof farm buildings could be realized. And so when Lenné pressed to extend the gardens established by Frederick the Great by buying and converting Charlottenhof he met with ready agreement.

King Friedrich Wilhelm III now demanded an expert report from Hofmarschall von Maltzahn by the cabinet order of 7 December 1825. His report was submitted directly to the king on 20 December. There is no doubt that Lenné had worked on it, and it is thus the first evidence of his single-minded determination to put the scattered royal and noble gardens around Potsdam together to form a large landscaped park that would go beyond the random limits set by history and topography. »I report to Your Royal Majesty ... about the forthcoming acquisition of the Charlottenhof estate; there is no doubt that joining this plot with the garden of Sanssouci would make a significant contribution to the beautification of this garden. The part of the garden containing the Temple of Friendship is very narrow. As this plot is now adjacent here, so the new parts of it would gain greater extent without great cost, but the gardens as a whole would gain significantly. For as long as the estate remains undivided in the hands of the present owner it will always remain a pleasant picture from the garden of Sanssouci and the acquisition will no be necessary; but because he must sell, as I have heard, ... it is very much to be feared that he would try to sell the same in small parcels, as in this way he would indisputably make the greatest use of it in this way in its proximity to Potsdam. But then the gardens around Sanssouci would probably be surrounded by vegetable gardens and cabbage patches, and thus this part of the garden would lose an infinite amount.«

The king bought the land, and the Crown Prince was given the site as a present at Christmas 1825, already accompanied by Lenné's preliminary plans, his own intentions and without any doubt at all by Schinkel's contract to rebuild.

The palace and park of Charlottenhof, which the Crown Prince called »Siam«, are different from the architectural dreams and visions of palaces and castles that concerned Friedrich Wilhelm IV throughout his life. The games of knights and water-sprites that the boy used to play with his brothers and sisters caused the rock fortress or the island monastery of »St. George in the Lake« rise from the waters of the Havel lakes; to the growing boy, swimming across the Potsdam Havel between Tornow and Hermannswerder with his brothers, a »Belriguardo« of longing appeared as a palace set high on the opposite bank; »Frau Minnetrost's Vantage-Point« towered into the sky on a steep hill before the eyes of the faithful reader of Fouqué; the Crown Prince, who was fighting for a worthy memorial for Frederick the Great, developed the monumental project of a »via triumphalis«, which was to enclose his great ancestor's garden like a historical panorama. Schloß Charlottenhof and its park were in pursuit of higher goals from the very start.

The Crown Prince counted Schinkel as one of his teachers, at least as far as architecture and drawing were concerned. Schinkel's instruction to the Crown Prince was always based on concrete examples from his practice. The prince accompanied the creation of the Charlottenhof park and palace with an unusually large number of sketches and plans, and esteemed his own part in the planning very highly. He spoke and wrote about »Siam« and even jokingly referred to himself as an architect from Siam at this time. A memo from Venice is signed »Architetto – Frederigo Siamese 1829«; even floor-plan drawings for suggested alterations to the Berlin Schloß and designs for the Prince Wilhelm's town palace, called midsummer night's dreams, carry signatures of this kind: »FW Siamhouse architect«, or all his pet names: »Fritz Siam Butt«.

Friedrich Wilhelm had adopted this name »der Butt« (the flounder) with a certain self-mockery and used the

sein Neffe Friedrich Wilhelm II. die Insel der Seligen auf Tahiti lokalisierte. In dem als tahitische Hütte gebildeten Turmkabinett seines Pfaueninselschlosses begegnen sich zwischen den Fenstern Darstellungen dieses Schlosses, des Marmorpalais im Neuen Garten und einer Insel Tahitis in der als Traumreich vorgestellten Seenlandschaft der Havel. Schließlich mag noch das von Friedrich Gilly errichtete Rohrhaus der königlichen Eltern in Paretz die Phantasie des Kronprinzen auf die Exotik als Gewand seiner Träume gelenkt haben.

Als die mit dem russischen Thronfolger Nikolaus verheiratete Schwester Charlotte 1817 nach Rußland abreiste, schrieb der Bruder ihr eine Abschiedsnovelle, *Die Königin von Borneo*. Er drückte darin Vorstellungen von Großherzigkeit aus, wie er sie den Weiten des Ostens, wohin die Schwester nun entschwand, angemessen glaubte. Im Geiste von Lessings Ringparabel erhoffte er den moralischen Triumph der Toleranz. Die Novelle war in Inhalt und Stil durch die orientalischen Verserzählungen *Lalla Rookh* von Thomas Moore angeregt, die der Kronprinz in der englischen Erstausgabe von 1817 zur Hand gehabt haben wird. *Lalla Rookh* diente am 27. Januar 1821 als Szenarium für ein Hoffest mit lebenden Bildern, Gesang und Tanz. Dabei verkörperte Prinzessin Charlotte (nunmehr Großfürstin Alexandra Feodorowna) die Titelgestalt, die indische Prinzessin Lalla Rookh, und spielte deren Brautfahrt nach Kaschmir nach, während Großfürst Nikolai ihren Bräutigam, den bucharischen Prinzen Aliris darstellte.

Siam, das arkadische Modell eines freien Landes, war mehr und anderes als ein Kronprinzentraum, es war für den Kronprinzen die eigene Besitzung, in der er seine Vorstellungen und die seiner künstlerischen und intellektuellen Berater von einem geordneten Gemeinwesen realisieren wollte. Die exotische Lokalisierung bot Möglichkeiten zum freien Einsatz architektonischer Metaphern ohne Bindungszwang an einen bestimmten Formenkanon. Schinkel, Lenné und der Kronprinz konnten die Fülle des Bildungsgutes ihrer Zeit aktivieren und daraus ein ikonographisches Programm aufstellen, in dem sich die Neigung Friedrich Wilhelms IV. zur Harmonisierung politischer und sozialer Kontraste ebenso ausdrückte wie sein Bewußtsein vom Offenhalten pragmatischer Lösungen. Hier wurde die Form gefunden, aus Architektur- und Gartenmotiven ein romantisches Staatsideal vorzustellen, das als Programmerklärung des preußischen Thronfolgers angesehen werden kann.

Lenné hat der Charlottenhof-Landschaft eine völlig autarke Gestalt gegeben. Zwar sind durch Auflichtungen und Neupflanzungen die Waldbezirke des friderizianischen Rehgartens jenseits des damals noch trennenden Parkgrabens einbezogen worden und lassen nach Norden die Illusion unendlicher Ausdehnung entstehen, doch im übrigen schließen dichte Gehölzstreifen die Außenwelt aus; nur nach Osten bleiben »geringe Andeutungen der Stadt Potsdam« zu ahnen. Ein großer, wie eine Parabel geführter Hauptweg, der im Bereich der ehemaligen Kunstmühle, der jetzigen Meierei, aus dem friderizianischen Garten kommt und in der Gegend des Freundschaftstempels dorthin zurückkehrt, umfaßt eine ideale Landschaft. Am südlichsten Punkt, am Zenit dieser Parabel, liegt das Schloß. Dort tangiert der Weg die architektonisch ausgebildete Schloßachse.

Alle von ihm ausgehenden Nebenwege führen ins Innere der modellhaften Weltlandschaft, die nach Os-

ten von Hügeln bewegt ist bis hin zur letzten Erhebung der Insel im Maschinenteich, während sie nach Westen in eine stille Ebene übergeht und an dem dichten Waldessaum endet.

Der als »Belt« ausgebildete Umfassungsweg führt im Osten von der damaligen Einmündung des Schafgrabens in den Parkgraben, den er mit einer Brücke überquert, auf den Komplex des Hofgärtnerhauses zu. Er steigt und fällt über die hügelige Modellierung des Geländes, so daß zuerst das Haus des Hofgärtners in den Blick gerät, dann die kleinen baldachinartigen Tempel über den Büsten der Eltern des Kronprinzen im Gedächtnisgarten hinter dem Haus, schließlich die Germanicus-Stele auf der Insel im Maschinenteich. Erst dann erreicht er die heute Römische Bäder genannte Anlage selbst.

Danach wendet er sich dem Schloß und seiner Terrasse zu mit der Blickrichtung auf dessen Gartenportikus, schwenkt aber, sobald er sich der Terrasse nähert, parallel zur Schloßachse auf das große Wasserbecken mit der Säule der Kronprinzessin ein und umgeht das Becken unterhalb der Terrasse.

Auch von Westen führte ursprünglich eine Brücke über den Parkgraben. Hier verläuft der Umfassungsweg vor dem abschließenden westlichen Waldrand und beschreibt einen großen Bogen um die jenseits am östlichen Rand der Gartenlandschaft liegenden Römischen Bäder, auf die sich unterschiedlichste Sichten ergeben, einmal nur auf das Gehilfenhaus, dann auf die ganze Ausdehnung der Anlage mit Einblick in den Gartenraum vor der Arkadenhalle. Schließlich erscheinen auch von dieser Seite Schloßterrasse und Schloß als Zielpunkt, das der Weg in direkter Konfrontation mit dem Halbzylinder der nördlichen Schmalseite und dem tempelartigen westlichen Portikus an dessen Nordwestecke erreicht.

Die traditionelle Nord–Süd-Erstreckung des 1825 von Friedrich Wilhelm III. für den Thronfolger erworbenen Gutshauses ermöglichte es Schinkel bei seinem Umbau des Gebäudes zum Sommersitz des Kronprinzen, dem Haus zwei völlig verschiedene Seiten nach Westen und nach Osten zu geben. Die über dem angeböschten Sockelgeschoß hochgestellte Westfassade verschließt sich mit ihrem repräsentativen Portal dem schnellen Zugang, während die eingeschossige Ostseite sich zur vorgelagerten Gartenterrasse darbietet. Doch ihr offener Portikus ist aus dorischen Säulen gebildet und daher von unüblichem Ernst; auch wahrt die Front durch die dazwischen gelegten Höfe Distanz und läßt nur die Durchsicht auf das goldgestirnte nachtblaue Oberlicht des Westportals zu.

Beide Seiten des Hauses sind Ausgangs- und Endpunkte von Gartenbezirken, die sich quer zu ihm zu einer Achse formieren. In der konsequenten Architekturgestalt dieser Schloßachse, die, von Ost nach West geführt, ein Bild des Tages- und Weltenlaufs bietet, ist ein Gleichnis für die Ewigkeit gefunden, in das der durch Eintritt in seine Geschichtlichkeit unsterblich zu denkende Mensch mit Gesetzen und Lebensregeln einbezogen ist. Der Aufbau dieser Achse erfolgte in mehreren Entwicklungsphasen; entscheidend war die Plazierung der »Feuermaschine« an ihrem östlichsten Punkt als Zeichen für den Sonnenaufgang und Beginn allen Lebens.

Als sich Schinkel 1827 nach seiner gemeinsam mit Peter Beuth unternommenen Englandreise entschloß, für den Betrieb der Fontänenanlagen von Charlotten-

4. Wilhelm Barth, Blick auf Schloß Charlottenhof, 1841. Ölgemälde. SPSG, GK I 6668.
5. August Wilhelm Ferdinand Schirmer, Blick von der Pergola des Schlosses Charlottenhof auf die Römischen Bäder, 1831. Ölgemälde. SPSG, GK I 2762. – Aus dem kleinen Portikus, wo die Pergola der Gartenterrasse am Schloß ansetzt, führt der Blick über die Voliere des unteren Hofes und zwischen den Säulen des großen Portikus auf die Gebäudegruppe um das Hofgärtnerhaus und das davorliegende Kulturstück.

4. Wilhelm Barth, view of Schloß Charlottenhof, 1841. Oil painting. SPSG, GK I 6668.
5. August Wilhelm Ferdinand Schirmer, view of the Roman Baths from the pergola of Schloß Charlottenhof, 1831. Oil painting. SPSG, GK I 2762. – From the small portico where the pergola meets the terrace by the Schloß the eye is carried over the aviary in the lower courtyard and between the columns of the large portico to the group of buildings around the court gardener's house and the orchard in front of it.

name »Butt« for his own portrait as a signature for selected drawings and when initialing letters and private communications. »Butt« was seen as a jocular adoption of the traditional title for the successor to the throne, as it has survived in the French »Dauphin«. »Ad usum delphini« was the name of the educational programmes compiled for the education of a future ruler. They ordered the entire knowledge of an age encyclopaedically and in a form that could be grasped by a young man. In Charlottenhof the name acquired symbolic significance. The service for use in the palace carries a golden flounder on a light blue ground on all its parts, surrounded by the letters »SIAM«; in the Roman Baths the flounder takes the form of a large, water-spewing fish: the master of the palace himself at the gardener's house as a »fons vitae«.

Siam, in the perception of the age the »Land of the Free«, was by no means an unusual name for an Arcadia or Utopia. The Electress and Queen Sophie Charlotte had already taken an interest in the distant country and discussed their reading of Simon de la Loubère's travel letters (*Du Royaume de Siam*, Amsterdam 1691) with Leibniz. The exotic quality of the Dutch territories in South America and China appealed more to the Great Elector as an alternative model to Europe. China and the fashion for China gave Frederick the Great the idea of building a garden pavilion, while his nephew Friedrich Wilhelm II places the Island of the Departed on Tahiti. Between the windows in the tower study, which was in the form of a Tahitian hut, in his Pfaueninsel palace, images of this palace, of the marble palace in the Neuer Garten and of a Tahitian island met in the lake landscape of the Havel, presented as a dream landscape. Finally the reed house built by Friedrich Gilly for the royal parents in Paretz may have drawn the Crown Prince's imagination to exoticism as the garment of his dreams.

When his sister Charlotte, who was married to Nicholas, the heir to the Russian throne, set off for Russia in 1817, her brother wrote her a farewell novel called *The Queen of Borneo*. In this he expressed ideas of magnanimity he considered appropriate to the world of the East, for which his sister was now departing. In the spirit of Lessing's parable of the rings he expected a great deal from the moral triumph of tolerance. The novel was inspired in content and style by Thomas Moore's oriental verse tales *Lalla Rookh*, which the Crown Prince will have had to hand in the first English edition of 1817. On 27 January 1821 *Lalla Rookh* served a the scenario for a court party with tableaux vivants, singing and dancing. In these the title role of the Indian princess Lalla Rookh was played by Princess Charlotte (now Grand Duchess Alexandra Feodorovna), who acted her bridal journey to Kashmir, while Grand Duke Nicholas played her bridegroom, the Bukharan prince Aliris.

Siam, the Arcadian model of a free country, was more than and different from a crown prince's dream. For the Crown Prince it was a possession of his own, in which he wanted to realize his ideas and those of his artistic and intellectual advisors of an ordered community. The exotic location offered opportunities for the free use of architectural metaphors without any compulsion to bind them to a particular formal canon. Schinkel, Lenné and the Crown Prince were able to activate the abundance of the educational store of their day, and build up an iconographic programme

from it that expressed Friedrich Wilhelm IV's inclination to harmonize political and social contrasts just as much as his awareness of keeping pragmatic solutions open. Here a form was found for presenting a romantic state ideal from architectural and garden motifs that can be seen as a declaration of the Prussian heir to the throne's programme.

Lenné gave the Charlottenhof landscape a completely self-sufficient form. It is true that the wooded areas of Frederick's deer-park beyond the Parkgraben, which that was still a dividing line at the time, are included by means of clearings and new plantations, producing an illusion that the estate stretches to infinity in the north, but elsewhere dense wooded strips shut out the outside world; only on the eastern side can »slight hints of the town of Potsdam« be detected. A large main path, running like a parabola, and coming out of Frederick's park in the area of the former power-driven mill, now the dairy, and turning back into it in the area of the Temple of Friendship, encloses an ideal landscape. At the southernmost point, the zenith of this parabola, is the palace. There the path touches the architecturally developed palace axis.

All the side paths branching out from it lead into the model-like world landscape, which is enlivened by hills to the east, down to the last rise of the island in the machine pool, while in the west it turns into a quiet plain, ending at the dense edge of the forest.

This enclosing path, developed as a »belt«, leads in the east from the point at which the Schafgraben used to join the Parkgraben, crossing it by means of a bridge, to the complex of the court gardener's house. It rises and falls over the hilly modelling of the site, so that first of all the eye lights on the court gardener's house, and the small, baldacchino-style temples over the busts of the Crown Prince's parents in the memorial garden behind the house, and finally the Germanicus stele on the island in the machine pool. Only here does it reach the area now known as the Roman Baths itself.

After this it turns towards the palace and its terrace, with the eye directed to its garden portico, but swings parallel with the palace axis as soon as it approaches the terrace towards the great pool with the Crown Princess's column and goes around the pool below the terrace.

A bridge originally led over the Parkgraben from the west as well. Here the enclosure path runs in front of the concluding western forest edge, describing a great curve around the Roman Baths on the other side at the eastern extremity of the park landscape. All kinds of different views are available of them over the broad expanse, in one case only of the staff building, then of the whole extent of the complex with a view into the garden room in front of the arcaded hall. Finally the palace terrace and the palace appear as a goal from this side as well. The path reaches the palace in direct confrontation with the half-cylinder of the northern narrow side and the temple-like western portico on its north-western corner.

The traditional north–south orientation of the farmhouse acquired by Friedrich Wilhelm II for the heir to the throne in 1825 meant that Schinkel, when he was converting the building into a summer residence for the Crown Prince, was able to give it two completely different sides to the west and the east. The west

hof die Dampfkraft einzusetzen, errichtete er im Osten, wo die Achse auf den erweiterten Schafgraben trifft, ein Haus für die »Feuermaschine« in Würfelform mit einem Aussichtsaltan. Das hatte die Ausdehnung der Ost–West-Achse nach beiden Seiten zur Folge. Zwischen der Feuermaschine und der Schloßterrasse entstand ein Rosengarten, auf den man vom Dach des Maschinenhauses Aufsicht hatte. Gleichzeitig wurde im Westen ein bis dahin noch nicht erworbenes Ackerstück angekauft und der Hippodrom projektiert.

Die Schloßachse beginnt am östlichsten Punkt der ganzen Anlage, am Ufer des Maschinenteichs, wo die Dampfmaschine die Elemente Wasser und Feuer zusammenbringt und von wo alle Bewegung ihren Ausgang nimmt. Vom Maschinenhaus konnte man das sich nach Westen erstreckende Gartenrechteck übersehen, das von dichten Fliederhecken eingeschlossen als Mittelpunkt eine rustikale Laube hat, die von konzentrischen Kreisen umgeben ist. Beiderseits querliegender vertiefter Rasenflächen eilt ein Wegepaar auf diese Kreise zu, deren überragende Ausweitung zum Innehalten veranlaßt. Von außen nach innen verengen sich die kreisenden Wege auf die Laube zu. Das Ganze ist ein Rosengarten nach dem Vorbild Humphry Reptons, der aber hier aus jahrhundertealter Motivtradition das biblische Paradies meint, dessen Rosenstöcke die Behausung des ersten Menschenpaares umgeben. Diese »Urhütte« leitet gleichermaßen einen architekturtheoretischen Exkurs über die Schloßachse ein, der vom Zelt, das die Exedra auf der Schloßterrasse bedecken sollte, und die Hausfassade des Gartenportikus zum Stibadium im Hippodrom führt.

Die Wege aus dem Paradies enden an der Substruktion der aufgeschütteten Gartenterrasse des Schlosses, deren im Halbkreis geführte rohe Ziegelmauer, welche die große Exedra trägt, durch Urnennischen als Grabesarchitektur charakterisiert ist. Der Aufenthalt im Paradies der Genesis ist nicht von Dauer. Auf den Genuß der Erkenntnis folgt die Sterblichkeit des Menschen. Eine steile Treppe bietet sich an, die Todesmauer zu überwinden. Sie ist streng in der Achse der darüberliegenden Pergola geführt, gewährt also nicht ein beliebiges Herankommen, sondern den Zwang, aufwärts zu steigen. Die Treppe führt zwischen zwei Plastiken hindurch: Apoll mit dem Köcher voller Pfeile, der dem Neuen, Jugendlichen, Bahn bricht, und Clio, die Muse der Geschichtsschreibung. Mit dem Wechsel der Generationen und dem Eintritt in die Geschichte kann der sterbliche Mensch unsterblich werden. Dann kann er auf der Höhe der Schloßterrasse in der großen Exedra auf den Gräbern Platz nehmen und urteilen. Er gewinnt den Blick gegen Morgen zum Gärtnerhaus und dem Italienischen Kulturstück, in dem die erfindungsreichen Gärtner tätig sind; zum gegenüberliegenden Mittagspunkt, dem Hügel mit der antiken Graburne, wo das Wasser in den am Boden gezogenen Wein floß und Auferstehung verhieß; und gegen Abend zur dunklen Kuppel des Neuen Palais, dem Zeichen von Geschichte und Vergangenheit.

Die Schloßterrasse bildet das Zentrum der durchgehenden Gartenachse. Sie beginnt im Osten mit der großen Exedra, von der aus die weite Parklandschaft, die Brunnen auf der Terrasse und das Haus betrachtet werden können. Hier ist der Platz, wo sich »der König ... ein zum irdischen Fatum erhobener Mensch« der Anschauung seines Volkes aussetzt, als das »Principium, welches alles umfaßt«, zur »organischen« Auflö-

sung des Gegensatzes von Herrschenden und Beherrschten (Novalis). In diesem Zusammenhang fällt auf, daß Schinkel in einem Blatt der *Sammlung Architektonischer Entwürfe* das Schloß Charlottenhof von der dem Gartenportikus gegenüberliegenden Rundbank aus zeigt: Auf der Bank sitzen zwei Männer, die eindeutig nicht den Bewohnern oder Gästen des Schlosses zugehören, sondern als Vorübergehende, als Wanderer charakterisiert sind, als Betrachter: »Sie genießen oder diskutieren den Anblick der Architektur ...« Dabei bietet sich ihnen zugleich die Möglichkeit, zu beobachten, wie sich der Hausherr, Kronprinz Friedrich Wilhelm (IV.), »in ... und um ... das Werk der Baukunst ... herum bewegen« würde.

Mit Rundbank und Gartenportikus begegnen sich hier die beiden Bestandteile des antiken Theaters, versteht man den Platz der Zuschauer, die Exedra, als verkürzte Form des Theaters und den Ort der Handelnden, den Portikus, als Scena. Schinkel begriff seine Architektur als »moralische Anstalt« und setzte dazu die auf der Schaubühne gewonnenen Fähigkeiten ein. Johann Gottfried Schadow hatte schon 1805 treffend bemerkt: »... befangen in dem ausgedehnten Raum einer Theater-Decoration ... glänzte (er) hiermit in einem Fache, welches die Architecten selten in dem Grad besitzen ...«

Schinkels Werk liefert für dieses Verständnis seiner architektonischen Motive erhellende Beispiele. Wenige Jahre vor der Planung von Charlottenhof schlug er für das Grabdenkmal des Fürsten Hardenberg an der Ostwand der Kirche zu Neuhardenberg eine Säulenarchitektur mit Dreiecksgiebel vergleichbar dem Gartenportikus von Charlottenhof vor, in der die Statue des zu Gedenkenden aufgestellt werden konnte – also eine Scena. Gegenüber ordnete er eine Exedra an, als Platz für sich an Hardenberg und sein Leben Erinnernde, gleichsam dem Erdenlauf des Verstorbenen Nachsinnende. Ganz ähnlich entstand wenige Jahre später eine solche Exedra auch am Familiengrab der Humboldts in Tegel. Neben dem archäologischen Wissen um das Theater der Antike steht dahinter die von den Denkmalen, Grabmälern, Theatern, Auditorien und Versammlungsstätten der französischen Revolutionsarchitektur ausgehende Faszination. Für ein Gleichnis des Augensinns galt Claude-Nicolas Ledoux' *Coup d'oeil du théâtre de Besançon*; für ein gebautes Symbol gespannter Aufmerksamkeit Jacques Goudoins 1769 errichtetes Amphithéâtre de l'École de Chirurgie, das unter anderem zum Prototyp nachfolgender Rauminstallationen für Volksvertretungen wurde.

Doch der Situation in Charlottenhof am nächsten kommt ein wirklicher Theaterentwurf Schinkels, der Plan zur Singakademie im Kastanienwäldchen hinter der Neuen Wache in Berlin von 1821. Grundriß und Schnitt durch diesen Bau zeigen das Gegenüber von Theater und Scena, verwandt bis zur Deckungsgleiche mit dem Plan der Gartenterrasse von Charlottenhof. Deutlich ist hier wie dort das Rund der Sitzbänke des Theaters (in Charlottenhof verkürzt auf die eine Rundbank) als Bereich der Zuschauer dem von Säulen markierten Aktionsraum der Handelnden gegenüber angeordnet. In der Singakademie erheben sich hinter der doppelten Säulenreihe die Stufen für die Chorsänger; in Charlottenhof öffnen sich zwischen den Säulen des Gartenportikus Einsichten in das Haus des Kronprinzen.

façade, placed high over the banked base storey, is closed to rapid access with its prestigious portal, while the single-storey east side opens on to the garden terrace in front of it. But its open portico is made up of Doric columns and thus unusually serious; the façade also keeps its distance as a result of the courtyards between, and it is possible to look through only a the night-blue, gold-starred skylight of the west portal.

Both sides of the building are entrances to and end points of garden areas that from an axis at an angle to it. The consistent architectural design of this palace axis, which, running from east to west, offers of view of how the day and the world are passing, provides an allegory for eternity in which man, to be thought eternal through his entry into history, is included with laws and rules for life. The structure of this axis emerged in several phases of development; a crucial feature was the placing of the »fire machine« at its eastern point as a sign of sunrise and the beginning of all life.

In 1827, when Schinkel decided, after his journey to England with Peter Beuth, to use steam to drive the Charlottenhof fountains, he built a cubic building with a viewing balcony for the »fire machine« to the east, where the axis meets the extended Schafgraben. A rose garden was created between the fire machine and the palace terrace, and there was a view of this from the roof of the engine house. At the same time, a piece of agricultural land that has so far not been acquired was bought and the hippodrome planned.

The palace axis begins at the easternmost point of the complex as a whole, on the bank of the machine pool, where the steam engine brings the two elements of fire and water together, and which is the start of all movement. The garden rectangle stretching out to the west and enclosed by dense lilac hedges and with a rustic arbour at its centre, surrounded by concentric circles, could be surveyed from the engine house. A pair of paths on both sides of diagonally placed lawn areas hurries towards these circles, forcing their movement to pause a little. The circling paths become smaller as they approach the arbour. The whole thing is a rose garden modelled on Humphry Repton, but here, based on a centuries-old motif tradition, it alludes to the biblical Garden of Eden, whose roses surrounded the accommodation of the first pair of human beings. This »primeval hut« effectively introduces an excursus in terms of architectural theory about the palace axis, starting with the tent intended to cover the exedra on the palace terrace and taking the building façade of the garden portico to the stibadium in the Hippodrome.

The paths from the Garden of Eden end at the substructure of the raised garden terrace of the palace, whose semicircular red-brick wall, which supports the great exedra, is characterized as tomb architecture. There is no lasting stay in the Garden of Eden. Human mortality follows enjoyment of the fruit of the Tree of Knowledge. A steep flight of steps is available for passing over the wall of death. It runs directly on the axis of the pergola above it, and thus makes it impossible to arrive randomly; one is compelled to climb upwards. The steps lead between two sculptures: Apollo with a quiver full of arrows, making a way for the new and youthful, and Clio, the Muse of History. Mortal man can become immortal with the changing generations and by entering history. Then he can sit down and make his judgement on the tombs in the great

exedra on the height of the palace terrace. He gains a view to the east, the morning, towards the gardener's house and the Italian Orchard in which the inventive gardeners are at work; to the midday point opposite, the hill with the ancient tomb urn where the water flowed into the vines growing on the ground, promising resurrection; and towards the evening in the west towards the dark dome of the Neues Palais, the symbol of history and transience.

The palace terrace forms the centre of the axis running through the garden. It begins in the east with the great exedra, from which the broad park landscape, the fountains on the terrace and the building can be observed. Here is place where »the King ... a human being raised to be an earthly fate« is exposed to the view of his people, as the »principium that includes everything«, to the »organic« dissolution of ruler and ruled (Novalis). It is striking in this context that Schinkel shows Schloß Charlottenhof from the round bench opposite the garden portico in a sheet of the *Sammlung Architektonischer Entwürfe*: Two men are sitting on the bench who are clearly not residents or guests in the palace, but characterized as passers-by, as wanderers, as observers: »They are enjoying or discussing the view of the architecture ...« At the same time they are also offered the opportunity of observing how the owner, Crown Prince Friedrich Wilhelm (IV), would »move in ... and around ... the architectural work«.

The two components of the ancient theatre meet here in the round bench and garden portico, if one sees the spectators' place, the exedra, as an abbreviated form of the theatre and the actors' place, the portico, as the scena. Schinkel perceived his architecture as a »moral institute« and used the abilities he had acquired in the theatre to this end. Johann Gottfried Schadow had remarked perceptively as early as 1805: »... enclosed within the extended space of a theatre set ... (he) shone in an area that architects seldom master to this degree ...«

Schinkel's work provides illuminating examples for this understanding of his architectural motifs. A very few years before Charlottenhof was planned he suggested columned architecture with triangular gables comparable with the Charlottenhof garden portico, in which the statue of the dead man could be placed for the tomb of Prince Hardenberg on the east wall of the church in Neuhardenberg – a scena, in other words. Opposite he arranged an exedra, as a place for those remembering Hardenberg and his life, thinking as it were about the earthly life of the dead man. In a quite similar way, a few years later an exedra of this kind was also created on the Humboldt family tomb in Tegel. Behind this, as well as archaeological knowledge about ancient theatre, is the fascination exerted by the monuments, tombs, theatres, auditoria and places of assembly of the French Revolution. Claude-Nicolas Ledoux's *Coup d'oeuil du théâtre de Besançon* stood as an allegory of sight; Jacques Goudoin's Amphithéâtre de l'École de Chirurgie, built in 1769, that became a prototype for subsequent spatial installations for representative bodies of the people, was a built symbol of eager attention.

But closest to the situation in Charlottenhof is a real theatre design by Schinkel, the plan for the Singakademie in the little chestnut wood behind the Neue Wache in Berlin, dating from 1821. Ground plan and section through this building show scena and theatre

Das Skulpturenprogramm auf der Gartenterrasse von Charlottenhof gibt zusätzliche Hinweise zum Sinn solcher Anordnung. Zu Seiten der Rundbank begegnen sich die Statuen von Hermes und Paris und deuten auf das Parisurteil hin: Hermes übergibt Paris die Aufforderung der Götter, zu urteilen, zu entscheiden und zu richten. Der Schäfer Paris, ein Landmann, ist herausgefordert, über Götter, seine Herren, zu befinden; Zeus sichert ihm seinen Beistand zu. Nicht von ungefähr tritt Hermes mit Pansflöte und Schwert als Argustöter auf.

Eine derart von den Betrachtern in der Exedra beim Haus des Kronprinzen eingeforderte Entscheidung konnte sich aber keineswegs allein auf die Architektur beziehen. Die auf der Rundbank Verweilenden sollten nicht vordergründig die Gegebenheiten der gebauten Welt genießen und diskutieren, sondern eingedenk deren »eigenthümlicher Eigenschaft« das Leben des Kronprinzenpaares auf dieser Bühne beobachten und beurteilen. Nimmt man die von Sonnenaufgang nach Sonnenuntergang orientierte Gartenachse als Verheißung ewiger Wiederkehr allen Lebens, dann ist das quer auf dieser Achse liegende Haus ein Gleichnis menschlichen Daseins an einem beliebigen Punkt des unaufhörlichen Kreislaufs: ein Tag in der Ewigkeit. Seinen Bewohnern obliegt es, nach den über ihre eigene Existenz hinaus ewig gültigen Gesetzen zu leben, durch Vorbildlichkeit die Normen des kategorischen Imperativs zu erfüllen – nicht als Selbstzweck, sondern den Vorübergehenden zur Belehrung. In der Nachfolge von Ledoux' Traktat *L'Architecture considérée sous rapport de l'art, des moeurs et de la législation* hat die aufklärerische Baukunst derartige Gedankenmodelle gebildet, um ein bestimmtes Denken und Verhalten ihrer Benutzer hervorzubringen.

Voraussetzung aber, zu wirken und »die Wirklichkeit ... auf den Gedanken« zu stellen, war, daß diese Gedanken entschlüsselt und gelesen werden konnten. Wie andere »sprechende« Grundmuster zitierte Schinkel daher auch Motive aus seinen Bühnenbildern. Damit nutzte er die Möglichkeit zu Anspielungen, mit denen er zumindest unter den gebildeten Zeitgenossen auf Verstehen rechnen konnte. Für Charlottenhof ergaben sich solche Motive vorzugsweise aus den Dekorationen zur *Zauberflöte* mit ihrem der Aufklärung dienenden maurerischen Ideengut; wohl auch, weil der Kronprinz sie besonders schätzte, vor allem aber wegen des Anliegens, der Postulate an das »Hohe Paar«. Angesichts des Schlüsselmotivs der Sternenhalle der Königin der Nacht verwundert es nicht, daß Schinkel diese Dekoration in der Folge ständig zitierte, wenn als Plafond eines Innenraumes das Himmelszelt oder der »gestirnte Himmel über uns« erscheinen sollte. In Charlottenhof erfolgten fragmentarische Hinweise an bedeutungsvollen Stellen: über dem Westportal als nachtblaues, goldgestirntes Oberlicht und als Himmelskuppeln über den Statuennischen des Gartensaals.

Das Schloß Charlottenhof erhebt sich für die Betrachter in der östlich gelegenen Exedra als Sarastros Tempel vor dem dunklen westlichen Himmel. Der Durchblick durch die Gebäudemitte ergänzt sich zur geschlossenen Sternenkuppel des Bühnenhintergrunds in der Eingangsszenerie der *Zauberflöte* mit dem Gegensatz von Tag und Nacht. In umgekehrter Richtung aber wußten die Charlottenhof-Betrachter die paradiesische Landschaft und den rauchenden

Vulkan aus der »IV. Decoration« in Gestalt des Rosengartens unterhalb der Exedra und des Kandelabers der »Feuermaschine« am Ufer des Maschinenteichs hinter sich. Die ägyptisierenden Rahmungen der drei Eingänge aus dem Gartenportikus in den Speisesaal charakterisieren die Situation als Sarastros Tempel in dieser Dekoration. Die drei Türen sind als die Eingänge zum »Tempel der Natur« rechts, zum »Tempel der Vernunft« links und zum »Tempel der Weisheit« in der Mitte zu verstehen.

Im Bühnenbild der *Zauberflöte* bezeichnete Schinkel die drei geschlossenen Tempeltore durch darüber aufgestellte Figuren – als »Weisheit« in der Mitte eine Osiris-Statue, als »Vernunft« links eine männliche Gestalt mit einer Schrifttafel, als »Natur« rechts eine Ziege. Analog erscheinen in Charlottenhof entsprechend attribuierte Einblicke und Durchsichten – an Stelle der Ziege ein Ganymed, durch den Portikus und die Eingangstür sichtbar aufgestellt in der rechten Ecknische des Saals; an Stelle des Helios-Sohnes Osiris die Lichtgestalt der Blumenampel im Saal; an Stelle der Figur mit der Schrifttafel, die den Fortgang der Geschichte anzeigt, ein David mit dem Haupt Goliaths in der Ecknische auf der linken Saalseite: Jugend, die das Alter überwindet.

Diese Dreiteilung entspricht auch der inneren Struktur des Schlosses, wie sie in seinem asymmetrischen Grundriß deutlich wird. Rechts liegt im nördlichen Teil des Gebäudes die mit ihrer Gruppierung der Räume um das mittlere gemeinsame Schlafzimmer in konventioneller Gebundenheit gegebene Wohnung des »Hohen Paares« als »Tempel der Natur«. Die beiden Wohnräume, von denen der westliche zugleich als Vorzimmer des Kronprinzen diente, legen sich wie ein Riegel vor die intimeren Räume der beiden Kabinette des Kronprinzen und der Kronprinzessin, die das Schlafzimmer rahmen. Das Schlafzimmer hat eine apsidiale Erweiterung erhalten, die als Halbzylinder vor die nördliche Seitenfront über die ursprüngliche Hausgrenze hinaustritt. Darin befinden sich drei Fenster mit unterschiedlichen Landschaftsausblicken, nach innen durch Pfeilerspiegel getrennt, die vom Boden bis zur Decke reichen und den geschlossenen Raum strahlenförmig in die die Welt symbolisierende Parklandschaft hineinziehen. Gleichzeitig werden dadurch die Fensterausblicke zu in den Raum als Lebensbereich hereingeholten Weltausschnitten. Damit ist auch auf die Aussage von Plinius, aus dem Speiseraum seines Laurentium hätte er Ausblicke auf drei Meere (»quasi tria maria prospectat«, *Briefe*, II, 17, 5), angespielt. Im gleichen Raum wird durch gegenüberliegende Spiegeltüren eine imaginäre Raumabfolge hergestellt, die sich zwischen den eigentlichen Schlafplatz, dem ein trennender Vorhang Erinnerung an einen Alkoven gibt, und die apsidialen Ausblicke legt. Ergaben im barocken Interieur gegenüberliegende Spiegel eine unendliche Raumerstreckung, für die dennoch ein Ende zu denken war, einen Einheitsraum, den man nur nicht bis zu seinem Ende übersehen konnte, so führt jetzt die Felderteilung der Türen zu einem konträren Effekt: Es erscheint ein unendliches Hintereinander absehbar endlicher Räume, immer neue Türen und Türen ohne Ende bis zu einer bedeutungsvollen »letzten Tür«. Der nach Raffael kopierte transfigurierende Christus über den Betten sichert jedoch die Verheißung zu, daß auf Schlaf wie Tod immer wieder eine Auferstehung folgen wird.

facing each other, and they relate to the plan of the Charlottenhof garden terrace to the point of congruency. It is clear that here and there the circle of seats in the theatre (abbreviated in Charlottenhof as the one round bench) is arranged as an area for spectators opposite the space allotted for the protagonists' action. In the Singakademie the steps for the chorus singers rise behind the double row of columns; in the Charlottenhof views into the Crown Prince's home open up between the columns of the garden portico.

The sculpture programme on the Charlottenhof garden terrace provides additional indications of the meaning of such an arrangement. At the sides of the round bench statues of Hermes and Paris meet, indicating the judgement of Paris: Hermes is handing Paris the gods' demand to assess, decide and judge. Paris, a shepherd, a countryman, is required to make a decision about gods, his lords; Zeus assures him of his support. It is no coincidence that Hermes appears as the killer of Argus, with pan-pipes and sword.

But a decision required in this way from the spectators in the exedra at the house of the Crown Prince could by no means relate only to architecture. The people sitting on the round bench should not enjoy and discuss the conditions of the built world superficially, but should observe and judge the life of the Crown Prince and Princess on this stage in awareness of their »peculiar quality«. If one takes this garden axis oriented from sunrise to sunset as a promise of the eternal return of all life, then the building lying across this axis is an allegory of human existence at a random point in the ceaseless cycle: a day in eternity. It is incumbent upon its residents to live according to the laws that are eternally valid over and above their own existence, and to fulfil the demands of the categoric imperative through exemplary behaviour – not as an end in itself, but for the edification of passers-by. After Ledoux's treatise *L'architecture considérée sous rapport de l'art, des moeurs et de la législation* Enlightenment architecture formed thought models of this kind in order to produce a certain kind of thinking and behaviour in the people who used it.

But if this was to work, and »reality« was to be placed »on the thoughts«, then it was essential that these thoughts should be decoded and read. Schinkel therefore cited motifs from his stage sets as well as other »eloquent« basic patterns. Here he was taking the opportunity to make allusions that could be understood by his educated contemporaries at least. For Charlottenhof he preferred his setting for *The Magic Flute* as a source for such motifs, with their stock of Masonic ideas providing enlightenment; probably also because the Crown Prince liked it particularly, above all because of the subject matter, the postulate to the »High Couple«. In view of the key motif of the Queen of the Night's starry hall, it is not surprising that Schinkel constantly quoted this setting subsequently when the firmament, or »starry heavens above us«, was to appear. In Charlottenhof fragmentary references to particular points resulted: as a night-blue skylight with golden stars above the west portal and as heavenly domes above the statue niches in the garden hall.

For the viewer, Schloß Charlottenhof rises as Sarastro's temples before the dark west sky in the exedra to the east. The view through the centre of the building becomes the closed starry dome of the stage background in the opening set for *The Magic Flute* with the contrast of night and day. But in the other direction observers of Charlottenhof were aware of the paradise landscape and the smoking volcano from the »IVth setting« in the form of the rose garden below the exedra and the candelabrum of the »fire machine« on the bank of the machine pool behind them. The Egyptian-style frames on the three entrances from the garden portico into the dining-room characterized the situation as Sarastro's temple in this stage setting. The three doors are to be perceived as the doors to the »Temple of Nature« on the right, the »Temple of Reason« on the left and the »Temple of Wisdom« in the middle.

In the stage set for *The Magic Flute* Schinkel identified the three closed temple doors with figures placed above them – a statue of Osiris in the centre as »Wisdom«, a male figure with an inscribed tablet, and a goat on the right as »Nature«. In the same way appropriately attributed insights and views appear in Charlottenhof – a Ganymede instead of a goat, placed in the right-hand corner niche of the hall so that it is visible through the portico and the entrance door; in place of Helios's son Osiris the light-figure of the hanging flowerpot in the hall; instead of the figure with the inscribed tablet, which indicates the forward progress of history, a David with a head of Goliath in the corner niche in the left-hand corner niche: youth conquering old age.

This division into three also corresponds with the inner structure of the palace, as is clear from its asymmetrical floor plan. On the right, in the northern part of the building is the residence of the »High Couple« as a »Temple of Nature«, conventionally restrained, in its grouping of rooms around a central common bedroom. The two living-rooms, of which the western one also served as the Crown Prince's anteroom, are placed like a bar in front of the more intimate small rooms for the Crown Prince and Crown Princess, and frame the bedroom. The bedroom has an apsidial extension that protrudes out beyond the original bounds of the building beyond the northern side façade, as a half-cylinder. In this are three windows with different landscape views, divided inside by pier glasses extending from floor to ceiling and drawing the closed space radially into the park landscape that symbolizes the world. At the same times the views from the windows become details from the world drawn into the room as a life-sphere. This is also an allusion to Pliny's statement that from the dining room of his Laurentium villa he had views of three seas (»quasi tria maria prospectat«, *Letters*, II, 17, 5). In the same room an imaginary spatial sequence is provided by opposite mirror doors placing itself between the actual sleeping area, which is reminiscent of an alcove because of its dividing curtain, and the apsidial views of the outside. In a baroque interior, mirrors placed opposite each other produced an infinite extension of space, but one for which an end was conceivable, a uniform space in which it was imply impossible to see to the end, but here the division of the doors' fields produces the opposite effect: an endless sequence of predictably finite rooms is produced one behind the other, always new doors and doors without an end, until a significant »final door« is reached. However, the transfigured Christ above the bed, copied from Raphael, secures the promise that, like death, sleep is always followed by an awakening.

Im südlichen Gebäudeteil links löst sich der Grundriß des »Tempels der Vernunft« zu freier Bestimmung der Räume auf. Kupferstichzimmer und Speisezimmer, auch Hofdamenzimmer, wechseln in Nutzung und Ausstattung. Man kann hier aus der Pergola direkt in das Schloß eintreten. Im vorgelegten kleinen Portikus geht man über das weißblaue Rhombenmuster des bayerischen Wappens, Huldigung an die Herkunft der Kronprinzessin, mit dem das Licht- und Schattenspiel in der Pergola in eine Kunstform übersetzt ist. Das folgende Eckkabinett mit seinen Ebenholztüren und Wänden in pompejanischem Rot zeigt Landschaften des Übergangs von Nord nach Süd, Gouachen aus Oberitalien und vom Oberrhein. Im Rückblick in die Pergola erlebt man eine Illusion des Südens, und die Achsenverschiebung zur Tür des nächsten Raumes macht die Wendung zum Fensterausblick auf einen nordischen Wald zwingend. Im Eckkabinett mit seinen ehemals von einem steingrauen Linoleum bedeckten Boden hat man die Gewißheit des sicheren Standes auf der gleichen Ebene wie in der Pergola draußen. Tritt man jedoch in das folgende Zeltzimmer ein, dessen Fußboden von einem wiesengrünen Linoleum mit Blumensträußen bedeckt war, dann verliert man diese Sicherheit, denn der Blick geht nun durch das Westfenster in die Baumkronen, während man durch das Südfenster im diagonalen Blick nach unten tief im Ungewissen den Wiesenraum der Parklandschaft wahrnimmt. Das Zelt als Bild der Lebensreise steht für die Offenheit aller Erwartungen.

Als »Tempel der Weisheit« in der Mitte vereinigen sich beide Tendenzen im freien Durchblick von Sonnenaufgang nach Sonnenuntergang: Die Existenz des Menschen berührt sich mit der Ewigkeit. Das warme Rot der Türbespannungen und der Vorhänge hinter den Statuen im Gartensaal entreißt der Ewigkeit einen Tag für die Gegenwart erfüllten Lebens. Dahinter öffnet sich die Tür ins Dämmerlicht des Vestibüls, das auf die Abendseite der großen Achse vorbereitet.

Jenseits des Hauses folgt ein Kastanienhain, dessen Bäume ursprünglich in der Form des antiken Quincunx standen. Es ist ein Hain der Erinnerung und des Träumens. Romeo träumte (nach Shakespeare) »in dem Schatten des Kastanienhains, der von der Stadt westwärts sich verbreitet«. Schinkel hatte bereits 1816–18 die Neue Wache in Berlin mit einem solchen Hain (»vor der Stadt gen Westen«) umgeben. Neben dem Gebäude waren Christian Daniel Rauchs Statuen der Generäle Scharnhorst und Bülow aufgestellt. Der entschlossene Heerführer Bülow und der gedankenvolle Planer Scharnhorst bildeten ein »komplementäres Paar von Gedanken und Tat« und brachten im Denkmalshain für die Helden der Freiheitskriege »Freiheit und Selbstentschließung« (Fontane) zum Ausdruck.

In Charlottenhof ist es ein Dichterhain. An seinen Eingängen stehen die Zeitgenossen Goethe, Schiller, Herder und Wieland in Richtung auf das Haus, ihnen entsprechen auf der Westseite die Dichter der Vergangenheit Ariost, Tasso, Dante und Petrarca, die in den Sonnenuntergang blicken. Im Dichterhain erinnert das Wasser, das die Gartenachse in ihrer ganzen Länge begleitet, an sein unterweltliches Wesen, denn hier hat es die Form eines Neptunbrunnens.

Im Osten pumpt die Maschine das Wasser aus dem Teich und drückt es in Röhren. Es taucht als Fontäne in der Urhütte auf, erscheint auf der Schloß-terrasse als Bild des altorientalischen Lebensbrunnens in Gestalt eines aufsteigenden Strahls, der in eine tröpfelnde Schale zurückfällt und durch Marmorkanäle wie in den Mogulgärten mit kleinen Seitensprudeln verbunden ist. Dann begegnete man dem Wasser wieder im Vestibül, wo es als Glockenfontäne aus einem Baluster aufstieg, der an die Wasserkandelaber der Pfaueninsel erinnert. Schließlich war eine Brunnennische vorbereitet für das Bad unter dem Schlafraum des Kronprinzenpaares. Den Abschluß bildete der Spiegel des Karpfenteichs und die Fontäne im Stibadium sowie drei runde Teichaugen, die das Oval des Hippodroms im Wald begleiteten.

Zwischen Dichterhain und Karpfenteich, der heute nur noch als schmales Rasenrechteck erhalten ist, liegt ein Rasengeviert, das mit Maiblumen bepflanzt war und wohl in der Sonnenglut einen betörenden Duft aussandte. Plinius berichtet von einer veilchenüberdufteten Terrasse im Laurentium (»violis oderatus«, *Briefe*, II, 17, 17).

Dem Morgenduft der Rosen im östlichen Paradies antwortet der Abendduft vor Sonnenuntergang. Denn nach dem Maiblumenstück versinkt die Sonne angesichts von Schlaf und Tod im Teich des Vergessens und hinter dem dichten Waldesdunkel. Das Schloß und der Dichterhain spiegelten sich im Wasserspiegel des Karpfenteichs, ebenso auch die als Schlaf und Tod verstandene, dahinter aufgestellte Ildefonso-Gruppe. Hinter der Gruppe schließt eine Heckenkonche im Halbrund die dichte, undurchdringliche Baumkulisse, die man nur auf versteckten Schlängelwegen durchdringen konnte.

Eine zeitgenössische Zeichnung von William Blake zeigt Virgil, der Dante ermutigt, einen solchen Wald zu durchdringen, um über Inferno und Purgatorio zum Paradiso zu gelangen. Das Dantesche Paradiso ist aber im Gegensatz zum vergänglichen Paradies der Genesis ein bleibender Ort, ein Elysium im Antikeverständnis der Renaissance. So liegt es auch am Ende und quer zur Achse des ewigen Ablaufs. Hier geht man nicht hindurch: man kommt an. Rosengarten und Hippodrom, gleichzeitig konzipiert und nacheinander entstanden, bezeichnen Beginn und Erfüllung der menschlichen Existenz, den Garten der Unschuld des ersten Paares und den Ort, wo sich die erfahrenen und geläuterten Seelen schließlich wiederfinden.

Irrend tauchte man aus dem Waldesdunkel wieder in einer Kunstform auf, dem querliegenden Oval des Hippodroms. Auf Lennés beiden ersten Plänen für Charlottenhof ist das Gelände als nicht zur Erwerbung gehörig ausgespart, in einem dritten Plan wird es noch als Fremdbesitz vermerkt. Im Plan von 1826 ist eine spätere Einzeichnung erfolgt, dabei wird das überkommene Grabensystem angegeben, das von Norden das Gelände umgreifend in zwei östlich und westlich gelegenen Ringgräben endet. Erst ein gesonderter Plan des Grundstücks im Jahr des Erwerbs 1835 diente der Planung des Hippodroms. Die sehr gedrungene, aus sechs in der Höhe ansteigenden Baumreihen und einer Beetkante um das innere Raumoval aufgebaute Form ist deutlich von Gabriel Thouin abhängig. Dessen Muster für eine Orangerie-Aufstellung ordnete von außen nach innen zwei Reihen Alleebäume, dann eine große plate-bande mit sehr großen Orangenbäumen, eine zweite mit mittleren Orangen, eine dritte mit sehr kleinen Orangen und eine innere plate-bande mit Blumen an – »ce qui ferait amphithéâtre«. Thouin bot fünf

In the southern part of the building on the left the floor plan of the »Temple of Reason« breaks up to define the spaces freely. The engraving room and dining room, also the room for the ladies-in-waiting, alternate in use and furnishings. Here you can enter the palace directly from the pergola. In the small portico in front of it you cross the blue and white rhomboid pattern of the Bavarian arms, a tribute to the origins of the Crown Princess, which changes the play of light and shade in the pergola into an art form. The subsequent small corner room with its ebony doors and walls in Pompeian red shows landscapes in the transition from north to south, gouaches from upper Italy and from the Upper Rhine. Looking back into the pergola you have an illusion of the south, and the shift of axes to the door of the next room makes it mandatory to turn and look through the window at a northern forest. In the small corner room with its floor formerly covered with a stone-grey linoleum one has the certainty of standing on the same plane as in the pergola outside. But when you go into the tent room that follows, whose floor was covered in meadow-green linoleum with bunches of flowers, then this certainty is lost, as the eye is now led through the west window into the crowns of the trees, while through the south window the lawns of the park can be made out uncertainly in the diagonal view down. The tent as a vision of the journey through life stands for the openness of all expectations.

As the »Temple of Wisdom«, both tendencies are drawn together in the free view from sunrise to sunset: human existence touches eternity. The warm red of the door coverings and the curtains behind the statues in the garden room seizes a day for the present time of fulfilled life from eternity. Behind this the door opens into the twilight of the vestibule, preparing us for the evening side of the great axis.

Beyond the building is a chestnut grove whose trees were originally in the ancient quincunx form. It is a grove of memory and of dreams. According to Shakespeare, Romeo dreamed »underneath the grove of sycamore that westward rooteth from this city side« – which in the German translation by August Wilhelm Schlegel, published in 1797, became a »grove of chestnut«. As early as 1816–18 Schinkel had surrounded the Neue Wache in Berlin with such a grove (»outside the town to the west«). Daniel Rauch's statues of Generals Scharnhorst and Bülow had been set up by the building. Bülow the decisive military leader and Scharnhorst the thoughtful planner formed »a complementary pair of thought and deed« and expressed »freedom and self-resolution« (Fontane) for the heroes of the Wars of Liberation in the memorial grove.

In Charlottenhof it is a poet's grove. At its entrances stand contemporaries Goethe, Schiller, Herder and Wieland facing the building, and corresponding to them on the western side are Ariosto, Tasso, Dante and Petrarch, poets of the past, looking into the sunset. In the poets' grove the water that accompanies the garden axis throughout its full length is reminiscent of its underworldly nature, as here it takes the form of a fountain of Neptune.

In the east the engine pumps the water out of the pool and into pipes. It comes up again as a fountain in the primeval hut, appears on the palace terrace as a symbol of the ancient oriental fountain of life in the form of a rising jet that falls back into a dripping bowl and is connected to small bubbling areas at the sides by marble channels, as in Mogul gardens. Then the water cropped up again in the vestibule, where it rised out of a balustrade like a bell fountain reminiscent of the water candelabrum on the Pfaueninsel. Finally a fountain niche was prepared for the bath under the Crown Prince's and Crown Princess's bedroom. The conclusion was the surface of the carp pond and the fountain in the stibadium and also three round pools accompanying the oval of the Hippodrome.

Between the poets' grove and the carp pool, which today has survived only as a small rectangular lawn, is a square of lawn that was planted with mayflowers and probably gave out a captivating fragrance in the glow of the sun. Pliny writes of a terrace fragrant with violets in the Laurentium villa (»violis oderatus«, *Letters*, II, 17, 17).

The evening fragrance before sunset responds to the morning fragrance of roses in the eastern paradise. For after the patch of mayflowers the sun, faced with sleep and death, sinks into the pool of oblivion and behind the dense darkness of the woods. The palace and the poets' grove were reflected in the surface of the carp pool, and so did the Ildefonso group, understood as sleep and death). Behind the group a semicircular half-dome hedge concludes the dense, impenetrable group of trees, which could be penetrated only on concealed winding paths.

A contemporary drawing by William Blake shows Virgil encouraging Dante to go through such a wood, in order to reach paradise via inferno and purgatory. But in contrast with the transient paradise of Genesis, Dante's paradise is a permanent place, and Elysium in the old perception of the Renaissance. And so it lies at the end of and sideways to the axis of the eternal sequence of events. You do not go through here, you arrive. Rose Garden and Hippodrome, conceived at the same time and created one after the other, define the beginning and fulfilment of human existence, the first couple's garden of innocence and the place where experienced and purified souls finally meet again.

Wandering around, one emerged from the dark wood into an art form again, the transverse oval of the Hippodrome. On Lenné's first two plans for Charlottenhof the area is separated off as not to be acquired, in a third plan it is still marked as owned by someone else. In the 1826 plan something else has been drawn in, and the inherited system of moats or ditches is indicated, running round the site from the north and end in two circular ditches to the east and west. It was only a separate plan of the site in the year in which it was bought, 1835, that shows the plans for the Hippodrome. The very squat shape, built up of six rows of rising trees and a bed edging the inner oval, is clearly dependent on Gabriel Thouin. His pattern for an orangery arranged two avenues of trees from outside to inside, then a large plate-bande with very large orange trees, a second with middle-sized orange trees, a third with very small orange trees and an inner plate-bande with flowers – »ce qui ferait amphithéâtre«. Thouin offered five paths running round between the rows of trees; these become three rows crossed by two transverse paths in Lenné's first design. A Charlottenhof plan drawn in the same year shows the original squat form with three paths running round it, which run into each other by using south-western and south-

umlaufende Wege zwischen den Baumreihen; drei Reihen, gekreuzt von zwei Querwegen, sind es in Lennés erstem Entwurf. Ein Charlottenhof-Plan des gleichen Jahres zeigt die anfänglich gedrungene Form mit vier umlaufenden Wegen, die mittels nordwestlicher und südöstlicher Schleifen ineinander übergehen. In einem nächsten Plan ist zum ersten Mal die neue Ost–West-Gartenachse von Charlottenhof in ihrer ganzen Länge vom Maschinenteich zum Hippodrom fixiert. Der Hippodrom hat bereits die gestreckte Form angenommen mit den deutlicher artikulierten Gebäuden an den Enden seines inneren Rechtecks, wie sie Schinkel in der Planung für das Antike Landhaus parallel entwickelte. Anstelle des Zugangsweges von Süden, der sich bei Schinkel wild durch den Wald schlängelt, wird bei Lenné der Hippodrom von vielen Seiten auf sehr ornamental geführten Wegen erreicht, und vor der Mitte der Westseite erscheint erstmals ein Ringgraben. Die endgültige Form des Hippodroms ist im folgenden Plan entwickelt. Jetzt sind drei Rundformen ausgebildet: zwei parallele Ringgräben westlich, ein mittlerer Rundteich östlich. Der Plan entwirft auch eine Gliederung und Ausweitung des Maiblumenstücks nach Norden und Süden mit Gartenteilen, die auf den mit Bleistift angedeuteten Schinkelschen Landhausentwurf antworten.

Im Einklang mit den Beschreibungen, die Plinius d. J. über seine Villen gab, war dieser Hippodrom niemals für Rennen und Pferdeläufe bestimmt, sondern sollte dem angenehmen Aufenthalt, der Kontemplation und Ruhe dienen (»sunt locis pluribus disposita sedilia e marmore, quae ambulatione fessos ut cubiculum ipsum iuvant«, *Briefe,* V, 6, 32–46).

Zu Recht hat man deshalb den Hippodrom mit Schinkels Rekonstruktionen dieser Villen in Beziehung gebracht, ebenso mit den Entwürfen für das Antike Landhaus westlich des Schlosses Charlottenhof. Das Antike Landhaus ist jedoch niemals gebaut worden. Angesichts der Tatsache, daß seine Planungsphasen in den entsprechenden Gartenplänen Lennés keine Spuren hinterlassen haben, darf man zumindest an Schinkels Realisierungsabsichten zweifeln.

Die Berufung auf Plinius reicht im Zusammenhang der Charlottenhof-Landschaft für eine Erklärung des Hippodroms als Gartenraum nicht aus. Seine umfassendere Bedeutung ergibt sich schon aus der parallelen Verlängerung der Achse von Osten nach Westen mit Rosengarten (1835) und Hippodrom (1836). Bringt man den Hippodrom von Charlottenhof in Beziehung zu Schinkels Lebenswerk, ergeben sich noch weiterführende Aspekte. Bei der Ausformung des Hippodroms begegnen sich Schinkel und Lenné in ihrem gemeinsamen Bezug auf Durand. In der ausgeführten Fassung der Hippodrom-Umgebung hat Lenné den Wasserring auf der Westseite des Hippodroms erhalten, ihm spiegelsymmetrisch einen zweiten hinzugefügt und beide durch einen Rundteich an der Ostseite ergänzt. Daraus ergab sich mit den drei Rundformen um das Oval ein von Durand als Nymphäon des Nero überliefertes Grundmuster.

Schinkel war nicht nur durch Friedrich Gilly auf die Adaption des Hippodroms als Ort von Volksfesten und Volksversammlungen vorbereitet. Er hatte in Rom die lebendigen antiken Überlieferungen erlebt, den Karneval und Wagenkorso auf der Piazza Navona, die Volksfeste in der Piazza di Siena im Garten der Villa Borghese. Friedrich Gilly könnte ihn hingewiesen haben

auf Friedrich Wilhelm von Erdmannsdorffs Hippodrom von 1775 im Lustgarten beim Dessauer Schloß, der tatsächlich als Reitbahn diente. Hier wurde der Reitunterricht für die Schüler des Philanthropins abgehalten, darüber hinaus war dieser Unterricht für alle Stände offen, brachte also auch das Prinzip der Volksvereinigung zum Ausdruck.

Die Architekten Mandar, Blondell und Cellerier richteten das Pariser Marsfeld für das erste große revolutionäre Fest am 14. Juli 1790 in Form eines Hippodroms ein, der den Triumphbogen aus drei Arkaden zum Einzug der Stände am Ufer der Seine mit einer Tribüne für die königliche Familie und die Deputierten an der Militärschule verband und in seinem Zentrum den »Altar des Vaterlandes« umschloß, an dem Talleyrand eine »patriotische Messe« zelebrierte.

Friedrich Gilly hat dieser Installation bei seinem Paris-Aufenthalt 1797 nachgespürt und die wenigen verbliebenen Reste in Zeichnungen überliefert. Offensichtlich reizte ihn der Vergleich mit seinem im Vorjahr konzipierten Entwurf zum Friedrichsdenkmal, dessen Grundriß der Hippodromform nahe steht.

Schinkel schlug 1814 für den gleichen Ort einen Dom als Denkmal für die Freiheitskriege vor. In der Planung des Areals erwies sich die Nähe beider Projekte. Schinkel wollte die überkommene barocke Platzanlage, das sogenannte Achteck, verlängern, so daß eine korrekte Hippodromform entstand, die sich im Anschluß an die zu erhaltenden Bauten der Ostseite des Achtecks aus drei auf Lücke gepflanzten Baumreihen bildete. Damit nahm er nicht nur die Form, sondern auch die patriotischen Ideen der Pariser Marsfeld-Formulierung auf, indem er die Vision einer Vereinigung von König und Volk mit der Totenehrung der Helden des Freiheitskrieges verband.

Bei der Lustgartenplanung im Zusammenhang mit der Errichtung des Museums in Berlin nahm Schinkel die Form wieder auf, um die urbanen Beziehungen zwischen dem alten Königsschloß und dem neuen Museum zu klären. Schinkel konfrontierte dem »dunklen« Schloß einen »hellen« Bildungstempel. Auf manchen Lustgartenveduten der Zeitgenossen ist zu erkennen, wie die besonnte südliche Front des Museums gegen die schattige Nordseite des Schlosses gestellt wird. Die Hippodromform bot sich als verbindendes Platzgefüge an. Der »Plan für Anordnungen der Pflanzungen im Lustgarten« vom Sommer 1828 sollte dem Platz ein »regelmäßiges Ganzes« geben, Schloß, Museum und Dom verbinden.

Der Kronprinz hatte regen Anteil an der Antikenrezeption, dem Studium der Briefe des jüngeren Plinius, an der Aufnahme der Renaissance und an der Lektüre von Dantes *Göttlicher Komödie,* von denen Schinkels Hippodromvorstellungen für Charlottenhof geleitet waren. Auch hatte er 1814 die Siegesparade der preußischen Truppen auf dem Pariser Marsfeld erlebt, von dessen Ort die demokratischen und patriotischen Ideen ausgingen, die Friedrich Gilly und Schinkel bewegten. Lenné brachte das gärtnerische, botanische und gestalterische Vermögen ein, das er der Belehrung unter anderem durch die Brüder Thouin in Paris dankte. Alles fügte sich zu der einzigartigen Gartengestalt zusammen, ohne daß sich die Anteile der Beteiligten auseinanderdividieren ließen, vielmehr bewahrt das bedeutungsvolle Oval in dem Waldstück westlich von Charlottenhof die geistige Polyvalenz seiner Schöpfer mitsamt ihrer erstaunlichen Gemeinsam-

eastern loops. In a subsequent plan, the new Charlottenhof east–west garden axis in its full length from the machine pool to the Hippodrome. The Hippodrome has already adopted its extended form with the more clearly articulated buildings at the ends of its inner rectangle, as developed by Schinkel for his parallel plans for the Antikes Landhaus. Instead of the access path from the south, which in Schinkel's case winds wildly through the woods, Lenné has the Hippodrome approached by very ornamental paths, and a circular moat appears before the centre of the western side for the first time. Now three circular forms have developed: two parallel ring moats to the west, and a central circular pool to the east. The plan also designs articulation and extension for the mayflower section to the north and south with gardens that respond to Schinkel's pencil sketch for the Landhaus.

Like the descriptions given by Pliny the Younger of his villas, this Hippodrome was never intended for racing and horses, but for spending time pleasantly, for contemplation and peace (»sunt locis pluribus disposita sedilia e marmore, quae ambulatione fessos et cubiculum ipsum iuvant«, *Letters*, V, 6, 32–46).

For this reason the Hippodrome was rightly associated with Schinkel's reconstructions of these villas, and also with the designs for the Antikes Landhaus west of Charlottenhof. The Antikes Landhaus was never built, however. Given the fact that there is no sign of its planning phases in corresponding garden plans by Lenné, Schinkel's actual intention to build is doubtful to say the least.

In the context of the Charlottenhof landscape it is not sufficient to appeal to Pliny for an explanation of the Hippodrome as a garden area. It can be fully explained only in terms of the parallel extension of the east-west axis by adding the Rose Garden (1835) and the Hippodrome (1836). If the Charlottenhof Hippodrome is then associated with Schinkel's life's work, aspects emerge that take us even further. In designing the Hippodrome, Schinkel and Lenné meet in their mutual relation to Durand. In the version of the area around the Hippodrome that was built, Lenné retained the circle of water on its western side, added a second one in mirror image and complemented both with a round pool on the east side. Three circles set around an oval: this was a basic pattern that had come down from Durand as Nero's Nymphaeion.

Schinkel was not only prepared by Friedrich Gilly for adapting the Hippodrome as a venue for popular festivals and assemblies. He had experienced lively ancient traditions in Rome, the carnival and carriage procession in the Piazza Navona, the popular festivals in the Piazza di Siena in the garden of the Villa Borghese. Friedrich Gilly could have pointed out Friedrich Wilhelm von Erdmannsdorff's 1775 hippodrome in the Dessau Schloß pleasure grounds to him, which actually was used for riding. Pupils at the Philanthropin were taught to ride here, and furthermore this teaching was available to all social groups, thus expressing the principle of popular unity.

Architects Mandar, Blondell and Cellerier arranged the Champs de Mars in Paris in the form of a hippodrome for the first great revolutionary celebration on 14 July 1790. It linked the triumphal arch with three openings for the entry of the estates on the banks of the Seine with a stand for the royal family and the deputies at the École Militaire. In the centre was the »Altar of the Fatherland«, at which Talleyrand celebrated a »patriotic mass«.

Friedrich Gilly had investigated this installation when staying in Paris in 1797 and drew the few surviving remains. Obviously he was attracted by the comparison with his own design for a memorial to Frederick, prepared in the previous year; the ground plan of the Hippodrome was close to this.

In 1814 Schinkel suggested a cathedral on the same site as a memorial for the Wars of Liberation. Plans for the area show how close the two projects were. Schinkel wanted to extend the survived Baroque square, the so-called Octagon, in order to produce a correct hippodrome shape. This was formed from three rows of trees planted in the gap and linking up with the buildings that were to be retained on the eastern side of the Octagon. Here he was adopting not just the form but also the patriotic ideas of the Champs de Mars formulation in Paris by combining the vision of unifying king and people with honouring the dead of the Wars of Liberation.

When planning the Lustgarten as part of the Berlin museum project Schinkel took this form up again in order to clarify the urban links between the old Berlin Schloß and the new museum. Schinkel confronted the »dark« Schloß with a »light« temple of knowledge. It is clear on many contemporary prints of the Lustgarten how the sunny southern façade of the museum is set against the shady northern side of the Schloß. The hippodrome shape suggested itself as an urban square structure that would combine and unite. The »plan for arranging planting in the Lustgarten«, dated summer 1828, was intended to make the square a »regular whole«, combining Schloß, museum and cathedral.

The Crown Prince was vigorously involved in the study of antiquity, in reading the younger Pliny's letters, in acceptance of the Renaissance and in reading Dante's *Divine Comedy*, all of which contributed to Schinkel's formal ideas for the Charlottenhof Hippodrome. He had also attended the Prussian troops' victory parade on the Champ de Mars in Paris in 1814, and this was the place from which Friedrich Gilly and Schinkel drew their patriotic ideas. Lenné contributed the horticultural, botanical and creative stock of ideas that he owed to the Thouin brothers in Paris, among others. All this joined to produce the unique garden design. It is not possible to identify the individual contributions made by those involved. On the contrary, the significant oval in the piece of forest west of Charlottenhof retains the spiritual polyvalence of its creators, together with their astonishing community of interest and unmistakable individuality.

»Once one has finally arrived in the Hippodrome one finds oneself surrounded by the crowns of the tall trees whose regular rows make up the Hippodrome, becoming lower the nearer to the centre they are. Inside they leave free a field, which is decorated on the one side by a stibadium, as Pliny called it. Here, under an arbour of vines, around a pool of water that is raised like a table, are several couches, which serve for the taking of a meal; on the other side of the Hippodrome, as a counterpart to the stibadium, is a salon with a small peristyle, in whose rear niche one can lie on couches and enjoy the foliage through the windows and the song of the birds, with the splashing of fountains in and around the building as an in-

keit und ihrer jeweiligen unverwechselbaren Individualität.

»Im Hippodrom endlich angelangt, sieht man sich von hohen Baumkronen umgeben, die in regelmäßigen Reihen den Hippodrom bilden und je weiter nach innen immer niedriger werden. Im Innern lassen sie ein Feld, welches an der einen Seite mit einem Stibadium, wie es Plinius nennt, verziert ist. Hier liegen unter einer Weinlaube um ein tischartig erhobenes Wasserbassin mehrere Ruhebetten, welche dienen ein Mahl einzunehmen; auf der anderen Seite des Hippodroms befindet sich als Pendant des Stibadiums ein Salon mit kleinem Peristyl, in dessen hinterer Nische man auf Ruhebetten das Laub durch die Fenster genießt und der Gesang der Vögel während des Plätscherns der Fontainen in und um das Gebäude zum Schlummer einladet. Der Mittelplatz des Hippodroms, der von Candelabern gut beleuchtet wird, ist für einen gesellschaftlichen Tanz bestimmt, der die Scene belebt.« (Karl Friedrich Schinkel, Erläuterungen zum Entwurf eines Antiken Landhauses).

Der Exedra im Osten, von der die beiden Wanderer das Schloß betrachten und den Eintritt der Sonne in den offenen Gartenportikus vor Augen haben, entspricht im Westen die Heckenkonche, aus der die marmornen Jünglinge der Ildefonso-Gruppe (*Castor und Pollux* oder *Schlaf und Tod*) durch den Schatten des Kastanienhains auf die verschlossene Tempelfront des kronprinzlichen Hauses sehen. Von der Morgenseite dringt das Leben in den Tageslauf des »Herrschers« ein; von der Abendseite kehren die auferstandenen Schatten der Geschichte zurück in seine exemplarische Existenz.

Hinter den Bäumen des Quincunx, die das Haus verdecken und nur den Blick auf seine Tempelmitte offenlassen, findet sich ein Warteplatz vor dem abweisenden Portal. Wenn es sich öffnet, gelangt man in das Vestibül, das zwischen den beiden Stockwerken des Hauses vermittelt. Es erinnert deutlich an das bereits erwähnte Vestibül eines römischen Hauses von Durand. Neben einer mittleren Fontäne leiten zwei seitliche Treppenläufe nach oben auf den Durchblick zum hochgelegenen Garten. Hinter der Fontäne führt eine schwere Tür in das verborgene Untergeschoß, darüber erscheint der Durchblick auf den freien Himmel mit dem hochaufsteigenden Wasserstrahl des Lebensbrunnens über der Gartenterrasse und der sonnendurchleuchteten Blumenampel. Die Ampel erinnert an den Engelsleuchter in Schinkels Mausoleum für die Königin Luise von 1810 und dessen ganz ähnliche räumliche Disposition, die darin auch die Ableitung von Krypta und hohem Chor romanischer Basiliken erkennen läßt. Denn die beiden Treppenläufe führen dort seitlich der tiefgelegenen Tür der Grabkammer auf das von einem Oberlicht mit außerirdischer Helligkeit erfüllte Podest für die Aufstellung des Sarkophages der Königin. Der Engelsleuchter symbolisiert das himmlische Licht ebenso wie die Blumenampel das irdische Sonnenlicht. Schinkel hat die Todessymbolik seines Frühwerkes umgewandelt in Lebenshoffnung.

Im Untergeschoß des Schlosses befanden sich die Wirtschaftsräume, Speisen- und Kaffeeküche und eine Milchkammer, die Wohnung der Kastellanin und der Raum für die Wache. Hinter der Schatztür des Vestibüls lag unter dem Gartenportikus die Silberkammer, unter dem Kupferstichzimmer hatte der Kronprinz eine Trinkstube mit an den Wänden umlaufenden illusionis-

tischen Landschaftsbildern und dem Ausblick in den Hof, der als Voliere diente; unter dem Schlafzimmer war eine Badestube vorbereitet, die durch die im Schrank des kronprinzlichen Kabinetts verborgene Treppe direkt zu erreichen war.

Bei der Einrichtung des Schlosses bestimmte Schinkel auch die Ausstattung der Innenräume bis ins Detail. Zu einigen Räumen zeichnete er die Entwürfe für das gesamte Mobiliar. In anderen Räumen arrangierte er bereits vorhandene Einrichtungsgegenstände, die nach einer wohl gemeinsam mit dem Bauherrn getroffenen Auswahl aus den Räumen des Kronprinzenpaares im Berliner Stadtschloß 1829 nach Charlottenhof überführt wurden. Für das Schlafzimmer des Kronprinzenpaares wurden zwei mit Adlern bekrönte, dekorativ vergoldete Holzsäulen wiederverwendet, die schon im Berliner Schloß für ein Bett der Kronprinzessin Elisabeth gedient hatten. Im Kabinett des Kronprinzen wurde in Reihe mit anderen Graphiken die Radierung von Carl Wilhelm Kolbe d. Ä. nach einer Gouache von Salomon Gessner, *La promenade sur l'eau*, gehängt, die als Vorbild für den überlaubten Kanal am Hofgärtnerhaus anzusehen ist. In einem Raum wechselnder Bestimmung kam ein bemerkenswertes Schreibmöbel zur Aufstellung, möglicherweise weniger um seinem Zweck zu dienen, als eine Haltung zu demonstrieren – wie das ganze Charlottenhof weniger ein bewohnbares Haus als vielmehr die Erklärung eines Programms sein wollte. Jener Schreibsekretär zeigt Schinkel in der Nachfolge der sogenannten Revolutionsarchitekten. Die französischen Architekten dieser Generation waren in der Mehrzahl durch Rom-Stipendien zu einer originären Rezeption der Antike gelangt und hatten daraus architektonische Autonomien von hohem philosophischen und moralischen Anspruch entwickelt. Friedrich Gilly übermittelte diesen Anspruch und dessen Formenkanon in den Zeichnungen seines Pariser Aufenthalts von 1797. Ihre kategorische Strenge erhält sich noch in den Adaptionen durch den jungen Schinkel, der die kubische Konsequenz der Quader und Würfel zunehmend durch scharfe Linearität für ihn charakteristischer Profile, Kanneluren, Palmetten und Voluten betont.

Das Äußere des Sekretärs ist dafür ein hervorragendes Beispiel. Ernst und ehrwürdig in den Formen eines antiken Monuments gebildet, offenbart das Möbel in geschlossenem Zustand nichts über seine eigentliche Funktion. Einem aufgerichteten Quader von im Verhältnis zu seiner Breite geringer Tiefe mit streng geschlossenem Umriß und nur mäßig verstärkter Sockelzone sind an der Vorderseite auf in Sockelhöhe hervortretenden Piedestals zwei durch straffe Kannelierung sehr schlank erscheinende Säulen vorgesetzt, die über fein ziselierten ionischen Kapitellen ein mächtiges vorspringendes Kranzgesims tragen. Die fest in sich ruhende Vertikalität, bestimmt durch das ausgeglichene Stütze-Last-Verhältnis von Sockel, Säulen und Kranzgesims, die Herbheit der Formen in Verein mit dem dunklen Mahagonifurnier und seiner über alles durchgehenden Maserung, bringt jenen Eindruck von Unnahbarkeit und fast monolithischer Abgeschlossenheit hervor. Zum Innehalten veranlaßt, nimmt man den sakralen Charakter dieses tempelartigen Äußeren auf, das allerdings keine Vorstellung eines Innenraums zuläßt. Vielmehr hat man durchaus die Empfindung von Monumentalarchitektur, von einem klassischen Andachtsmal, wie es die römischen Gräberstraßen belegte und

9. Carl Wilhelm Kolbe d. Ä., *La promenade sur l'eau*, nach einer Gouache von Salomon Geßner von 1775, 1806. Radierung. Erschienen im 2. Heft der *Tableaux en gouache, demi-gouache et dessins en lavis de Salomon Gessner, gravées à l'eauforte par W. Kolbe*, Zürich 1805/11. – Das Blatt hängt seit 1829 im Kabinett des Kronprinzen im Schloß Charlottenhof.
10. Karl Friedrich Schinkel, erster Entwurf zum Hofgärtnerhaus und Teepavillon am Maschinenteich. Bleistift auf blauem Tonpapier. SMPK, SM 51/16.

9. Carl Wilhelm Kolbe the Elder, *La promenade sur l'eau*, after a gouache by Salomon Geßner dating from 1775, 1806. Etching. Appeared in the second number of the *Tableaux en gouache, demi-gouache et dessins en lavis de Salomon Gessner, gravées à l'eauforte par W. Kolbe*, Zürich 1805/11 – The sheet has hung in the Crown Prince's private room in Schloß Charlottenhof since 1829.
10. Karl Friedrich Schinkel, first design for the court gardener's house and the tea pavilion by the machine pool. Pencil on blue-toned paper. SMPK, SM 51/16.

vitation to slumber. The central point in the Hippodrome, which is well lit by candelabra, is intended for a social dance, which enlivens the scene.« (Friedrich Schinkel, explanations of his design of an Antikes Landhaus)

The exedra in the east, from which the two wanderers are looking at the palace and see the sun entering the open garden portico, is balanced in the west by the hedge half-dome, from which the marble youths of the San Ildefonso group (Castor and Pollux or Sleep and Death) look through the shadows of the chestnut grove to the closed temple façade of the Crown Prince's house. From the morning side, life penetrates the »ruler's« daily routine; from the evening side the resurrected shadows of history move back into his exemplary existence.

Behind the trees of the quincunx, which conceal the building and leave only the view of its temple-centre open, a waiting place is to be found in front of the forbidding portal. When it opens, you are taken into the vestibule that links the two storeys of the building. This is clearly reminiscent of the above-mentioned vestibule for a Roman house by Durand. Two staircases at the side of a central fountain lead up to the view of the garden, which is placed higher. Behind the fountain a heavy door gives access to the hidden lower storey, and above this a view of the open sky with the high water-jet of the fountain of life above the garden terrace and the hanging flowerpot with the sun shining through it. The flowerpot is reminiscent of the angel chandelier in Schinkel's 1810 mausoleum for Queen Luise, which has very similar spatial disposition, showing a clear relationship with crypt and high choir in Romanesque basilicas. In the mausoleum the two staircases lead on either side of the deep-set door to the tomb chamber to the platform intended for the Queen's sarcophagus, which is flooded with heavenly light from a skylight. The angel chandelier symbolizes heavenly light in the same way that the hanging flowerpot symbolizes earthly light from the sun. Schinkel has transformed the death symbolism of his early work into hope for life.

The basement area of the palace accommodated domestic facilities, kitchen for food and coffee and a dairy chamber, the chatelaine's rooms and a guardroom. The strongroom for silver was behind the treasury door in the vestibule; under the engraving gallery the Crown Prince had a drinking parlour with illusionistic landscapes all round the walls and a view of the courtyard that served as an aviary. Under the bedroom was a bathroom that could be reached directly via a concealed staircase from the cupboard in the Crown Prince's private room.

When fitting out the palace Schinkel decided on the furnishings for the interior rooms, down to the last detail. He designed all the furniture for some of the rooms. In other rooms he arranged existing furniture that had been sent from the Crown Prince's and Princess's rooms in the Berlin Schloß to Charlottenhof in 1829, probably after consultation with his client. Two decoratively gilded wooden columns topped with eagles were re-used for the royal bedroom; they had been used in the Berlin Schloß for Crown Princess Elisabeth's bed. In the Crown Prince's small private chamber an etching by Carl Wilhelm Kolbe the Elder after a gouache by Salomon Gessner, *La Promenade sur l'eau*, was hung with a series of other prints; this

can be seen as the model for the canal bridged by foliage by the court gardener's house. A remarkable writing desk was placed in one room used for general purposes, possibly less to serve its purpose than to demonstrate an attitude – just as the whole of Charlottenhof was less a house to live in than a demonstration of a programme. This bureau shows Schinkel as a successor to the so-called revolutionary architects. The majority of French architects of this generation had experienced antiquity at first hand through scholarships to Rome, and had developed independent architectural theories with high moral and philosophical claims from this. Friedrich Gilly transferred these claims and this formal canon into the drawings he made while staying in Paris in 1797. This categorical austerity survives in adaptations by the young Schinkel, who increasingly emphasized the cubic consistency of the cuboids and cubes by the sharp linearity of the profiles, fluting, palmettes and volutes that were so typical of him.

The exterior of the bureau is an outstanding example of this. It has the earnest and venerable forms of an ancient monument, and when closed reveals nothing of its actual function. Two columns, which are made to appear very slender by tight fluting, are placed in front of an upright cuboid that is very shallow in relation to its width; its outline is austerely solid and the base area only moderately larger than the rest. The columns stand on pedestals that protrude at the front at the level of the base, and support a massive, forward-thrusting cornice above finely chased Ionic capitals. The harmonious vertical quality, determined by the balanced support-load relationship of base, columns and cornice, the astringency of the forms working with the dark mahogany veneer, with its grain running through everything, produces that impression of unapproachability and almost monolithic isolation. Compelled to pause, one takes in the ecclesiastical character of this temple-like exterior, which certainly admits no idea of an interior. On the contrary, the entire impression is one of monumental architecture, of a classical devotional monument of the kind found in Roman streets of tombs and that sentimental landscape gardens set by their delicate paths. The front of the cuboid, which is only lightly articulated, fits in with this as well. Its upper part is defined by the golden section, and the double framing with corner palmettes encloses an area that seems as if intended for an inscription.

It is not until the bureau is used that this area is seen to be the underside of the writing flap, which folds down. In contrast with the distancing vertical quality of its exterior the bureau opens up into the inviting horizontal of a Gothic hall that extends right across the entire upper surface: the ancient shades of the exterior open to reveal an interior bathed in bright sunlight. Four miniature clustered piers in light maplewood support three Gothic arches filled with delicate tracery above their impost profile. The fields underneath are divided into two on both sides by a respond; the central one is opened as a reflected niche to an uncertain depth and appears to continue the hall in all directions. The link between interior and exterior is sustained throughout: the light Gothic piers correspond with the dark Ionic columns, the shallow base, massive arches and the central niche of the hall correspond with the base area, cornice and opening of

wie es der sentimentale Landschaftsgarten an seine empfindsamen Wege versetzt hat. Dem entspricht auch die nur ganz flach gegliederte Vorderseite des Quaders, in dessen durch den goldenen Schnitt bestimmten Oberteil die doppelte Rahmung mit eingefügten Eckpalmetten eine Fläche umschließt, die wie für eine Inschrift vorgesehen erscheint.

Erst wenn das Möbel in Gebrauch genommen wird, erweist sich diese Fläche als Unterseite der herausklappbaren Schreibplatte. Der Sekretär öffnet sich im Kontrast mit der distanzierenden Vertikalität seines Äußeren zur einladenden Horizontale einer quer über die ganze obere Fläche sich erstreckenden gotischen Halle: Das antikisch verschattete Außen enthüllt ein in hellem Sonnenlicht strahlendes Innen. Vier miniaturhafte Bündelpfeiler aus hellem Ahornholz tragen über ihrem durchlaufenden Kämpferprofil drei Spitzbogenarkaden, die mit zartem Maßwerk gefüllt sind. Die Felder darunter werden beiderseits von einem Dienst zweigeteilt, das mittlere ist als verspiegelte Nische in unbestimmte Tiefe geöffnet und scheint die Halle nach allen Seiten fortzusetzen. Der Bezug zwischen außen und innen ist über alle Teile durchgehalten: die hellen gotischen Pfeiler entsprechen den dunklen ionischen Säulen, der flache Sockel, die mächtigen Arkaden und die Mittelnische der Halle entsprechen Sockelzone, Kranzgesims und Öffnung des Ganzen. Das Spiel von außen und innen findet sich auch in der hellen Mosaikmusterung der Schreibfläche, die wie das Pflaster eines Hofes vor der Arkadenhalle liegt, und in den sternförmigen Rhomben der Bodenfläche in der Mittelnische, die wie der Fußboden eines über die Sockelzone erhöhten Raumes wirken.

Es erscheint aber beim Gebrauch die Hand des Schreibenden in der Spiegelnische. Sie löst sich dabei von ihrem konkreten Subjekt und dem banalen Vorgang und wandelt sich zum Genius des Schreibens, zum Symbol der Kommunikation in jenem »tintenklecksenden Säculum«. So kann die Dreierarkade mit ihrer herausgehobenen mittleren Öffnung auch als Altaraufsatz empfunden werden, der in seiner Mittelnische dem Allerheiligsten Raum gewährt. Denn es ist das Schreiben, dem dieser Altar errichtet wurde.

Vergleichbares findet sich bei Georg Friedrich Kersting in dem Tag und Nacht, aktives und kontemplatives Tun des Menschen symbolisierenden Bildpaar in Weimar: *Kügelgen am Schreibtisch* (1811) und *Der elegante Leser* (1812). Der in hellem Tageslicht gegebene Kügelgen sitzt, vom Rücken gesehen, schreibend an seinem Arbeitsplatz. Man wird ausführlich über ihn unterrichtet durch das auf und über dem Schreibtisch aus Utensilien des Künstlers – Zeichen- und Schreibgeräten, ein Muskelmann als Studienobjekt und Gipsabgüsse – arrangierte »Weltensemble«. Es charakterisiert den Dargestellten als einen aktiv Tätigen, bei dem sich die Aneignung der Welt durch zeichnerische oder schreibende Produktion seiner Hand vollzieht. Zwischen den Fenstern, schräg über dem Rücken des Sitzenden, hängt ein Spiegel, in dessen rechter unterer Ecke der auf dem Schreibtisch liegende Gipsabguß einer Hand derart gespiegelt wird, daß sie wie schreibend erscheint. Der Spiegel wird zum Fokus der Tätigkeit des Porträtierten. Gleichzeitig wirkt die bleiche Gipshand wie eine Geisterhand, ein Menetekel der über dem Tun des Menschen verrinnenden Zeit.

Schinkels Schreibmöbel birgt eine weitere Überraschung. Nimmt man es als Mikrokosmos seines architektonischen Œuvres, dann scheint neben Antike und Gotik das ossianische Element zu fehlen, Widerhall der Kastelle des Nordens, der wehrhaften Bauten der Normannen. Doch noch ist die breite Stirnfläche des großen Kranzgesimses zu öffnen. Herausgezogen und ausgeklappt, ergibt sie ein leicht geneigtes Pult in bequemer Stehhöhe. Auch dieses Innen ist hell vom Holz der Silberpappel, die Pultfläche wiederum mit einer als Hofpflaster zu denkenden Mosaizierung, aber die niedrigen Stirnseiten als rustifizierte Mauerflächen grau abschattiert mit seitlichen alkovenartigen Rücksprüngen. Nicht lockere Heiterkeit des ungehemmten Schreibens im Sitzen ist hier angezeigt, sondern die Ernsthaftigkeit amtlicher Korrespondenz und Prüfung.

Nun könnte es scheinen, als biete die Kühnheit der Schinkelschen Erfindung – mehr noch die ihr folgende Deutung – nur ein Möbel für die Idee des Schreibens, ungenügend für praktische Zwecke. Nichts davon: einmal geprüft, erweist der Sekretär seine in der Nutzung aller Möglichkeiten ebenso kühne Konsequenz. Schon von außen offenbart er restlose Raumausnutzung, das gesamte Volumen des Quaders von der Schreibklappe abwärts wird von drei großen Schubkästen ausgefüllt, deren unterster den ganzen Sockel einnimmt. Hinter der geöffneten Klappe schlagen die Seitenwände der gotischen Halle als Türen tiefer Fächer auf, die ganze Arkadenzone läßt sich mittels einer Teleskopaufhängung als großer Schub herausziehen, schließlich springt dem Kundigen der Sockel zu drei Geheimfächern auf. Auch die normannische Mauermitte im Stehpult zeigt sich als breiter Schubkasten, die Rücksprünge daneben bilden offene Ablagefächer, hinter denen, herausgezogen, ebenfalls tiefe Schübe erscheinen; und wiederum läßt der richtige Druck auf das Vorfeld der wehrhaften Mauer dieselbe zu vier unterschiedlichen Breschen mit inneren Behältnissen aufspringen. Dieses reiche Innenleben ist schon in den Inventarien-Anzeigen des Jahres 1826 geschildert. Schinkel meinte zu solchen Gegenständen, daß sie ihrem Zweck vollkommen entsprechen müßten, aber auch die Idee dieses Zwecks vollendet zum Ausdruck zu bringen hätten.

Es ist üblich geworden, die gesamte Gebäudegruppe, die Karl Friedrich Schinkel ab 1829 als Hofgärtner-Etablissement zum Schloß Charlottenhof errichtete, als Römische Bäder zu bezeichnen. Ursprünglich verstand man unter diesem Namen nur den letzten Teil der Anlage, eine spielerische Adaption der durch aktuelle Grabungen in Pompeji vermittelten Kenntnisse antiken Hausbaus. Das Ganze hat mit dem Bau des Hofgärtnerhauses begonnen, in dem auch die Appartements für Gäste des Kronprinzen untergebracht waren. Dazu gehört ein Turm mit dem Reservoir für die Gartenbewässerung und darunter einem Badekabinett sowie die Wohnung für den Gehilfen über dem Kuhstall. Ein Tempel am Wasser diente dem Kronprinzen als Teepavillon; die gegenüberliegende Arkadenhalle bot von ihrem Dach eine weite Aussicht.

Anfangs wollte Schinkel die Hofgärtnerwohnung in der Pumpstation für den Park Charlottenhof unterbringen. Lenné hatte dafür bereits an der südöstlichen Parkgrenze einen Hügel errichtet. Die Bauform war durch den Turm des Reservoirs und den auf hoher Kante stehenden Quader bestimmt, in dem »ein vierfüßiges Tier« das gewaltige Tretrad bedienen sollte.

the whole. The interplay of interior and exterior is also found in the light mosaic patterning of the writing surface, which is placed in front of the arcaded hall like the pavement of a courtyard, and in the stellar rhomboids of the floor area in the central niche, which seem like the floor of a room raised above the base zone.

Only when the bureau is used the hand of the person who is writing appears in the mirror niche. In doing so it is detached from its concrete subject and the banal process and transformed into the genius of writing, into the symbol of communication in that »scribbling century«. In this way the trio of arches with its emphasized central opening can also be seen as an altarpiece granting space to the holy of holies in its central niche. For it is to writing that this altar was built.

Something comparable can be found in pair of pictures in Weimar by Georg Friedrich Kerstin symbolizing day and night, active and contemplative human activity: *Kügelgen am Schreibtisch* (1811) and *Der elegante Leser* (1812). Kügelgen is presented in broad daylight, seen from behind, writing at his desk. We are informed about him in detail by the »world ensemble« arranged on and above the desk. It is made up of artist's equipment – writing and drawing utensils, a student's model of a man's muscles, and plaster casts. This identifies the subject as an active person, for whom the world is acquired by drawing or writing with his hand. Between the windows, diagonally above the seated man's back, hangs a mirror in the bottom right-hand corner of which the plaster cast of a hand lying on the desk is reflected in such a way that it appears to be writing. The mirror becomes the focus of the subject's activity. At the same time the pale plaster hand seems like the hand of a ghost, a portent of time trickling away above the doings of mankind.

Schinkel's desk conceals another surprise. If it is taken as a microcosm of his architectural œuvre, then one element seems to be missing alongside the ancient and Gothic worlds: the Ossianic element, an echo of northern fortresses, the Normans' fastnesses. But the broad face of the great cornice can be opened as well. When pulled out and folded down it forms a slightly sloping desk at a comfortable standing height. This interior too is bright with the wood of the silver poplar, and the desk surface is once again provided with a mosaic covering that could be seen as the paving of a courtyard. However, the low ends are shaded in grey as rusticated masonry surfaces, with returns like alcoves at the sides. This does not indicate the relaxed cheerfulness of uninhibited writing when sitting down, but the serious nature of official correspondence and examination.

Now it could seem that the boldness of Schinkel's invention – and even more the interpretation that followed – offered only a piece of furniture for the idea of writing, inadequate for practical purposes. No sign of this: once tested, the bureau shows how consistently it exploits every possibility. Even from the outside it reveals that the space is used to the greatest possible extent. The whole volume of the cuboid from the writing-flap downwards is taken up with three large drawers, the lowest of which occupies the entire base. Behind the open flap the side walls of the Gothic hall open up as doors to deep compartments; the whole arched area is suspended telescopically and can be pulled out as a great drawer, and finally the base springs open to reveal three secret compartments for those in the know. The Norman masonry at the centre of the high desk also turns out to be a wide drawer, and the returns beside it form open storage spaces, behind which deep drawers appear when they are pulled out; and again the correct pressure on the area in front of the defensive wall causes four different gaps with internal containers to spring open. This lavish interior life can be seen even in the inventory notes of 1826. Schinkel thought that such objects should be entirely appropriate to their purpose, but they should express the idea of that purpose perfectly as well.

It has become customary to refer to the entire group of buildings that Karl Friedrich Schinkel built as a court gardener's establishment for Schloß Charlottenhof from 1829 as the Roman Baths. Originally this name referred only to the last section of the complex, a playful adaptation of knowledge of ancient building practice acquired from contemporary excavations at Pompeii. The whole thing had started with the building of the court gardener's house, which also contained apartments for the Crown Prince's guests. This included a tower with the reservoir for garden irrigation and under this a bath-house and accommodation for the staff. A temple by the water served as the Crown Prince's tea pavilion; the arcaded hall opposite provided a wide-ranging view from its roof.

At first Schinkel intended to accommodate the court gardener in the pumping station for Charlottenhof park. Lenné had already constructed a mound for this on the south-eastern boundary of the park. The shape of the building was determined by the reservoir tower and the cuboid reserved for »a quadruped« that was to work the massive treadmill. The view of this long building already shows the characteristic features of the later court gardener's villa. A tower and one long low and one short high building are placed together on a longitudinal axis, with a transverse pergola attached to the latter. A carriage house anticipates the later position of the lakeside pavilion in relation to the house. The site could be seen as a counterpart to the existing old court gardener's house (the dairy converted by Ludwig Persius) at the north-eastern corner of the site.

After the decision to use steam power, a new site was found for the court gardener's house on the bank of the Schafgraben between the machine pool and the diary. This position meant that the buildings, when seen from the Charlottenhof terrace, seemed to be among the Roman ruins of Frederick the Great's mound of ruins in Sanssouci, which at that time could still be seen above the treetops. At first the longitudinal composition was retained on the final site as well, but then the building was placed sideways to the villa. The court gardener's house now followed, in detail and type, the free-standing, post-antique Italian farmhouse made up of horizontal and vertical stone slabs with flat shed roofs over open roof trusses, surrounded by vine arbours, the kind of building that has always fascinated northern visitors to Italy.

Preparing his Italian journeys had brought Schinkel to address the problems of combining buildings with their natural surroundings, something that had scarcely been considered by the architectural theory and practice of his day. »On a journey through the Italian mainland and its islands I took the opportunity of collecting a quantity of interesting works of architecture that hitherto have been neither considered nor very much used. ... In doing this I set myself the task of se-

Die Ansicht des langgestreckten Gebäudes zeigt bereits die charakteristischen Motive der späteren Hofgärtnervilla. Ein Turm sowie ein langer niedriger und ein kurzer hoher Baukörper sind auf eine Längsachse gereiht, an letzteren schließt sich eine quergelegte Pergola an. Ein Wagenschuppen nimmt im Verhältnis zum Haus die spätere Position des Pavillons am See vorweg. Der Standort könnte als Pendant zum vorhandenen alten Hofgärtnerhaus (der von Ludwig Persius umgebauten Meierei) an der Nordostecke des Geländes verstanden werden.

Nach der Entscheidung für die Dampfkraft wurde für die Wohnung des Hofgärtners ein neuer Ort am Ufer des Schafgrabens zwischen Maschinenteich und Meierei gefunden. Diese Position ließ die Bauten von der Charlottenhof-Terrasse gesehen unter den römischen Ruinen des friderizianischen Ruinenberges von Sanssouci erscheinen, die damals noch über den Baumwipfeln zu erkennen waren. Auch am endgültigen Standort wurde zuerst die Längskomposition beibehalten, dann aber der Baukörper der Villa quergestellt. Das Hofgärtnerhaus folgte nun in Gestalt und Details dem Typ des freistehenden nachantiken italienischen Bauernhauses aus liegenden und stehenden Quadern mit flachen Pultdächern über offenen Dachstühlen, umgeben von Weinlauben, wie alle Italienfahrer aus dem Norden stets fasziniert hat.

Die Vorbereitung seiner Italienreisen hatte Schinkel auf die Probleme der Verbindungen von Bauwerken mit ihrer natürlichen Umgebung geführt, die von der Architekturtheorie und -praxis seiner Zeit noch kaum beachtet worden waren. »Auf einer Reise durch das feste Land Italiens und seine Insel fand ich Gelegenheit eine Menge interessanter Werke der Architektur zu sammeln, die bis jetzt weder betrachtet noch sehr benutzt werden. ... Ich setze mir dabei vor, Gegenstände von ausgezeichneter Art zu wählen, ich nehme mir diesem Zwecke zu Folge die Freiheit einzelne Theile welche an einem wirklich vorgefunden Gegenstande gemein und ohne Character stehen gegen andere an dem selben Ort gefundene bessere zu vertauschen, um dadurch an dem einen Gegenstand das Interesse zu vermehren.« Mit der Schilderung und Analyse eines Landhauses bei Syrakus formulierte er seine Ansichten über freie räumliche Kompositionen von Gewachsenem und Gebautem für die erste Fassung eines geplanten eigenen *Architektonischen Lehrbuchs*.

Der ländliche Charakter des Hofgärtnerhauses wird wesentlich durch die Anordnung von Sattel- und Pultdächern über offenem Dachstuhl hervorgerufen. Auch derartige Dächer und ihre Kombinationen hat Durand zusammengestellt. Im Vergleich ist klar zu erkennen, mit welcher geistigen und formalen Souveränität Schinkel die von Durand vorgeprägten Muster für seine eigenen Vorstellungen einzusetzen verstand.

Über die Herkunft des Turmes als bestimmender Vertikale der Römischen Bäder gibt Schinkels Zeichnung des Klosters San Lorenzo fuori le Mure in Rom von 1803 Auskunft. Sie läßt sein Studium formaler und räumlicher Beziehungen ebenso erkennen wie die Suche nach einem verbindlichen rechtwinkligen System als Grundlage des Zusammenfügens unterschiedlicher Elemente zu einer malerischen Silhouette. Aus dieser Bereicherung seiner Kenntnisse planerischer Möglichkeiten erwuchs die meisterhafte Komposition der ganzen Anlage, wo sich um den Angelpunkt des Turms

Kuben und Freiräume, geschlossene und durchsichtige Glieder auf unterschiedlichen Ebenen zu einer vollendeten dreidimensionalen Erscheinung ordnen.

Auch das Motiv des Pavillons am See geht auf ein verbreitetes Italienerlebnis zurück. Die Tempelform übernahm Schinkel aus James Stuarts und Nicholas Revetts *Antiquities of Athens*, denen er auch andere griechische Vorbilder verdankt. Doch das für die Teegesellschaften des Kronprinzen eingerichtete Interieur steht in überraschendem Gegensatz zu der Tempelform. Drei Fenstertüren der Stirnseite führen auf eine festliche Vorfläche unter weißblauem Oberlicht, das die Lichtreflexe auf das Wasser von Maschinenteich und Graben aufnimmt. Die beiden Fenster in den äußersten Enden der Südwand lassen dagegen den Blick direkt auf die bis an die Außenmauer anstehende Teichfläche stürzen, während die gegenüberliegenden Fenstertüren der Nordwand ohne Verbindung untereinander in den großen Garten oder in die Pergola führen, so daß sich vier gänzlich getrennte Ausblicke ergeben.

Der Pavillon ist eine Herrschaftsarchitektur im Gärtnerbezirk, er korrespondiert als soziale Verschränkung der Stände mit dem bäuerlichen Trogbrunnen am ursprünglich unter einer aufgestützten Linde bestehenden Sitzplatz der Gärtner beim Schloß.

Die dortige repräsentative Aufstellung der Büste der Kronprinzessin auf einer hohen Säule wie ein alles regelnder Schattenstab findet seine zweifellos emanzipatorisch gemeinte Antwort im Amazonenthema des Pavillons. Amazonensäule, ägyptisierender Kamin und Gemäldeauswahl mit der Kopie von Schinkels *Blick in Griechenlands Blüte* bieten im Teepavillon einen Mikrokosmos der geistigen Welt des Kronprinzen. Hinter dem Tempel liegt ein kleiner Gartenhof, der aus der östlich des Hofgärtnerhauses verlaufenden Pergola zu erreichen ist. Er entstand 1835 als Gedächtnisgarten. Unter Baldachinen stehen hier die Büsten der Eltern des Kronprinzen, Friedrich Wilhelm III. und Luise; am Sockel der Königsbüste erinnert eine Texttafel an dessen Aufruf von 1813. Von der Exedra zwischen den Baldachinen geht der Blick auf das sonnenbeschienene südliche Rosenspalier am Hofgärtnerhaus. Nach Osten liegt vor dem Tempel eine umschlossene Terrasse. Sie führt zu der Laube, die sich über dem Schafgraben wölbt. Der überlaubte Schafgraben eröffnet dem Kahnfahrer die Wasserweite des Maschinenteiches. Auch aus den Südfenstern des Tempels hat man Aufsicht auf dieses große Wasser, ohne es aber erreichen und vorbei an der Insel seine Ausdehnung ins Ungewisse übersehen zu können. Das Motiv der Laube über den Schafgraben stammt aus der philanthropischen Bilderwelt des Kronprinzen. Für eine frühe Darstellung der Römischen Bäder, die noch eine von der Ausführung abweichende Form des Gärtnerhauses und eine auffallend schmale Erstreckung des Gartenraumes annimmt, hat die Radierung von Carl Wilhelm Kolbe vorgelegen; die Gruppe der Kahnfahrer ist von Schinkel fast wörtlich übernommen. Die Spannung aus dem Verlangen nach unbekannter Ferne und gleichzeitiger Geborgenheit beherrscht die Anlage in vielen Punkten. »Dazu gehört gleich wohl, daß man dahingegangen sei, daß man zurück muß, daß man hinüber möchte, daß man es nicht kann, daß man alles zum Leben vermißt und die Stimme des Lebens dennoch ... vernimmt ...« (Heinrich von Kleist). Auch aus dem großen Gartenhof läßt sich das spüren, doch

lecting objects of an excellent kind. As a consequence of this purpose I permit myself the liberty of exchanging individual parts that stand meanly and without character on an object that I have really found for better ones found in the same place, thus increasing interest in the one object.« In this description and analysis of a country house near Syracuse he formulated his views on free spatial compositions made up of established, built work for the first version of a planned *Architektonisches Lehrbuch* of his own.

The rural nature of the court gardener's house is invoked essentially by the arrangement of gable and shed roofs over an open roof truss. Durand also assembled roofs of this kind and their combinations. In comparison it soon becomes clear with what intellectual and formal mastery Schinkel saw how to use the patterns established by Durand for his own ideas.

Schinkel's drawing of the monastery of San Lorenzo Fuori le Mure in Rome, dating from 1803, provides information about the origin of the tower as the defining vertical for the Roman Baths. It reveals his study of formal and spatial relationships just as much as his search for definitive rectangular system as a basis for fitting different elements together to form a picturesque silhouette. The masterly composition of the complex as a whole arose from this enrichment of his knowledge of design possibilities: cubes and open spaces, closed and transparent elements on different levels come together to form a complete three-dimensional phenomenon around the corner-point of the tower.

The motif of the lakeside pavilion goes back to a familiar Italian experience as well. Schinkel took over the temple form from James Stuart's and Nicholas Revett's *Antiquities of Athens*, which he also has to thank for other Greek models. But the interior designed for the Crown Prince's tea parties provides a surprising contrast with the temple form. Three french windows at the end lead to a festive forecourt under a blue-and-white skylight that takes up the reflected light from the machine pool and the moat. But the two windows in the outer end of the south wall give a direct view of the pool surface, which extends right up to the outer wall, while the french windows in the north wall opposite lead either into the large garden or the pergola, so that four completely different views are produced.

The pavilion is architecture for a ruler in the garden sphere. As a means of tying the estates together socially it corresponds with the rustic trough fountain by the gardeners' sitting area at the palace, under a propped-up lime tree.

The representative placing of a bust of the Crown Princess there on a tall column, like a shadow bar regulating everything, finds a response, which is doubtless intended to be emancipatory, in the pavilion's Amazon theme. In the tea pavilion, an Amazon column, a fireplace in the Egyptian style and the selection of paintings, including a copy of Schinkel's *Blick in Griechenlands Blüte* (View of Greece's burgeoning) offer a microcosm of the Crown Prince's intellectual world. Behind the temple is a small garden courtyard that can be reached from the pergola running east of the court gardener's house. It was planted as a memorial garden in 1835. Busts of the Crown Prince's parents, Friedrich Wilhelm III and Luise, are to be found here, under baldacchinos; an inscribed plate on the plinth of

the King's bust records his 1813 appeal. From the exedra between the baldacchinos there is a view of the sunlit rose trellis on the court gardener's house. East of the temple is an enclosed terrace. It leads to the arbour that arches out over the Schafgraben, which, with foliage arching over it, opens up the broad waters of the machine pool to boating parties. There is a view of this large watercourse from the south windows of the temple as well, but it is not possible to go down to it and form a view of intent extending into the unknown past the island. The motif of the arbour above the Schafgraben comes from the Crown Prince's world of philanthropic images. Carl Wilhelm Kolbe's etching was available for an early depiction of the Roman Baths, which still uses a form of the gardener's house that differs from the one built, and shows a remarkably small area of garden; Schinkel has taken over the group of people in a boat almost literally. The tension between longing for unknown distances and yet feeling secure at the same time dominates the complex in many ways. »Part of this is probably that one has gone there, that one has to get back, that one would like to cross over, that one cannot do it, that one is lacking everything for life and yet can still ... hear the voice of life ... « (Heinrich von Kleist) This can be sensed from the great garden courtyard as well, but here the view is tied to a north–south axis, which one experiences form the depths of the ancient rooms behind the arcaded hall. It leads through the impluvium, the atrium, the garden fountain and the stele of Germanicus on the island to the uncertainties of the water, where it meets the east–west axis of the palace.

Schinkel's intended »ceaseless pleasure ... in continued extent and enrichment« came into being north of the arcaded hall. Rooms were built around the atrium that had originally been planned in a loose sequence intended to express the idea of the Pompeian house simultaneously with ancient themes. It was only on a second attempt that the fountain niche behind the arcaded hall was transformed into an antique vestibule with an impluvium behind it and the apodyterium, which ended in three half-domes. On the left, a caldarium with a sunken bathing pool under the skylight, in front of this a billiard room, also lit from the top, and on the right a viridarium with an intimate garden court, complemented by the waterside colonnade. The garden court, the arcaded hall, which was perceived as a coloured tent, the atrium and the impluvium establish a rapid sequence of spaces moving from light to dark and back to light again. »Thus this complex forms a whole, grouped picturesquely, offering manifold pleasing views, secret resting places, comfortable rooms and open spaces for the enjoyment of rural life, by nature capable of continuing expansion and enrichment, so that a ceaseless pleasure in production is reserved.«

Seen from the west, looking down the side of the garden from north to south, are the staff house, the water-tower, the court gardener's house, the lakeside pavilion and the little courtyard with the baldacchinos for the busts of the Prince's parents. The different buildings are held together by a large arbour of the kind frequently noted by Schinkel on his journey to the south in Italy and Sicily. In searching for asymmetrical architectural compositions he had been particularly interested in the arbour as an intermediate form consisting of a built framework filled with something or-

ist hier die Aussicht an eine Nord–Süd-Achse gebunden, die man aus der Tiefe der antiken Räume hinter der Arkadenhalle erlebt. Sie führt über Impluvium, Atrium, Gartenfontäne, Stele des Germanicus auf der Insel ins Ungefähre der Wasserfläche, wo sie sich mit der Ost–West-Achse des Schlosses trifft.

Das von Schinkel vorgesehene »unausgesetzte Vergnügen ... fortgesetzter Ausdehnung und Bereicherung« vollzog sich nördlich der Arkadenhalle. Um das ursprünglich vorgesehene Atrium wurden in lockerer Folge Innenräume gebaut, die die Idee des pompejanischen Hauses zugleich mit der antiker Thermen ausdrücken sollten. Erst in einem zweiten Anlauf wandelte sich die Brunnennische hinter der Arkadenhalle zu einem antikischen Vestibül mit dahintergeordnetem Impluvium und dem in drei Konchen endenden Apodyterium, zur Linken ein Caldarium mit vertieftem Badebecken unter dem Oberlicht, davor ein ebenfalls von oben erhelltes Billardzimmer und zur Rechten ein Viridarium mit intimem Gartenhof, vervollständigt vom Säulengang am Wasser. Der Gartenhof, die als farbiges Zelt gefaßte Arkadenhalle, Atrium und Impluvium bilden eine schnelle Folge vom Hellen zum Dunklen und wieder Hellem wechselnder Räume. »So bildet diese Anlage ein malerisch-gruppiertes Ganze, welches mannigfaltige angenehme Ansichten, heimliche Ruheplätzchen, behagliche Zimmer und offene Räume für den Genuß des Landlebens darbietet, und seiner Natur nach immer fortgesetzter Ausdehnung und Bereicherung fähig ist, so daß daran ein unausgesetztes Vergnügen der Produktion vorbehalten bleibt.«

In der Ansicht von Westen bieten sich dem Blick über die Seite des Gartens von Norden nach Süden gereiht das Gehilfenhaus, der Wasserturm, das Hofgärtnerhaus, der Pavillon am See und der kleine Hof mit den Baldachinen für die Büsten des Elternpaares. Die unterschiedlichen Bauteile sind von einer großen Laube vereint, wie sie Schinkel auf der Reise nach dem Süden in Italien und Sizilien mehrfach notierte. Denn bei der Suche nach asymmetrischen Architekturkompositionen hat ihn die Laube als Zwischenform von gebautem Gerüst und gewachsener Füllung im kompositorischen Gleichgewicht mit dem Kubus des Hauses besonders interessiert. Bei der Darstellung dieser Westansicht findet sich unter den Wiedergaben der Römischen Bäder in der *Sammlung Architektonischer Entwürfe* das Blatt mit zwei Wanderern, doch sie betrachten nicht Bauwerk oder Bewohner, sondern bewegen sich selbst in der Architektur – sie ersteigen die Treppe im Hintergrund der großen Laube. In der gegensätzlichen Charakterisierung der beiden Wanderer auf den Zeichnungen vom Schloß und den Römischen Bädern – einmal als urteilende Zuschauer, zum anderen als handelnde Personen – stellte sich Schinkel dem Widerspruch aus Kontemplation und Aktivität, der seine Zeitgenossen bewegte, und um den Goethe im Monolog des *Faust* rang. In der festen orthogonalen Fassung des Schloßbezirkes hatte er eine anschauliche Gestalt für das »Wort« gefunden, während die »mannigfaltige Gruppe architektonischer Gegenstände« um die Römischen Bäder zur »Tat« herausforderte. Er deutete die Polarität von Schloß und Gärtnerhaus als ein sich wechselseitiges Bedingen von Bewahrung ewig gültiger Gesetze durch einen »Herrscher, der überall auf der Höhe der Bildung steht und sich demgemäß umgibt«, auf der einen und »fortgesetzter Ausdehnung und Bereicherung ... so daß

daran ein unausgesetztes Vergnügen der Production vorbehalten bleibt« auf der anderen Seite. Im Gegensatz zum Schloß, »mannigfach und doch Eins« (Friedrich Wilhelm IV.) steht die ungezwungene und freie Entwicklung der Umgebung des Hofgärtnerhauses. Das System gleichzeitiger offener und gebundener Ordnung von Bauten, Freiräumen, vorgegebenen Richtungen und willkürlicher Bewegung, die amtlichen und privaten Beziehungen zwischen Kronprinz und Hofgärtner, zwischen herrschaftlichen Gästen und Wanderern, Meistern und Gehilfen, der Hauswirtschaft des Hofgärtners und herrschaftlichen Gesellschaftsbezirken wirken wie eine idealisierende Verklärung des Ständewesens, gewachsener und überlieferter Regeln im Zusammenklang mit ewigem Fortschreiten und ständigem Wandel.

In der großen Laube bildet die Treppe ein Kernstück der Komposition, die ihrerseits die heterogenen Bestandteile der Gebäudegruppe der Römischen Bäder zusammenhält. Schinkel hatte eine solche gegenläufige Treppe bei seiner ersten Italienreise in einem Bauerngehöft in Anacapri erlebt und gezeichnet. Die damalige Zeichnung dürfte Grundlage mehrerer Skizzen Schinkels und des Kronprinzen zur Herausbildung der Gestalt der Römischen Bäder gewesen sein. Gegenläufige Treppen sind ein altes Motiv des Aufstiegs aus dem Dunkel zum Licht; so findet man sie in ägyptischen Tempelanlagen, auf Darstellungen des Babylonischen Turms, schließlich in Entwürfen zum Denkmal Friedrich des Großen von Heinrich Gentz und Friedrich Gilly. Analoge Bedeutung hat die Treppe in Schinkels Dekoration zur *Zauberflöte*. Hier dient sie als Ort der Läuterung von Tamino und Pamina: Am Ende des Prüfungsweges durch Feuer- und Wasserhöhle erhebt sie das Paar in das Licht von Sarastros Tempel.

Der Sitzplatz unter der großen Laube ist ein bacchischer Ort. Zwei kolossale Dionysoshermen tragen das Gebälk, hinter dem Marmortisch zeigt Christian Daniel Rauchs Relief ein Bacchanal, flankiert von Pan- und Satyr-Tondi; auf der halbhohen Mauer stehen Mischgefäße ebenfalls mit bacchanalischen Szenen. Ein Ort also, der den Wanderer zur Rast lädt, ihm in Korrespondenz mit dem gegenüberliegenden Vorbau des Kücheneingangs zum Hofgärtnerhaus Stärkung durch Speise und Trank verspricht; mit Blick auf den Überfluß an Früchten und edlen Gemüsen im Italienischen Kulturstück auch zu üppigem Gelage ermuntert. Doch Schinkel ließ (nicht nur auf der Zeichnung) die Wanderer hier nicht verweilen. Der ganze Bereich unter der großen Laube symbolisiert den Weg der Läuterung vom Genießen zum Emporsteigen (Bacchus/Dionysos) und der Entscheidung zwischen Wollust und Tugend (Herakles). Dionysos und Herakles, die dem Zeus von sterblichen Müttern geboren wurden, verdienten sich den Olymp nur durch diese Läuterung und Entscheidung. Der Weg beginnt bei dem als Brunnentrog dienenden Sarkophag unter der vorderen Herme, auf der ein bärtiger Dionysos als »Weinspender« bezeichnet ist. Wasserspendender Fisch und Muschel erinnern an die Verbundenheit des Dionysos mit Meer und Unterwelt, das Kentaurenrelief auf dem Sarkophag an den von übermäßigem Weingenuß ausgelösten Streit zwischen Kentauren und Lapithen. Die den Sitzplatz, aus dessen Tisch ebenfalls eine kleine Fontäne sprudelt, begrenzende zweite Herme trägt einen jugendlichen Dionysos, an dessen Stirnband Flügel sitzen; er ist als »Beflügelnder« bezeichnet. Unter

ganic, balanced in terms of composition with the cube of the house. Among the renderings of the Roman Baths in the *Sammlung Architektonischer Entwürfe*, the sheet with two wanderers appears as the depiction of the western view. However, they are not looking at the building or the people who live in it, but moving within the architecture themselves – they are climbing the steps behind the large arbour. In his contrasting characterization of the two walkers in the drawings of the palace and the Roman Baths – once as judging spectators, then as active participants – Schinkel was addressing the contradiction between contemplation and activity that exercised his contemporaries, and with which Goethe was wrestling in the *Faust* monologue. He had found a vivid form for the »word« in the strict, right-angled setting for the palace, while the »manifold group of architectural objects« around the Roman Baths was a challenge to the »deed«. He interpreted the polarity of palace and gardener's house as a mutual interdependence of preserving eternally valid laws through a »ruler who was at the pinnacle of education in all things and who determines his surroundings accordingly« on the one hand and »continuing expansion and enrichment, so that a ceaseless pleasure in production is reserved« on the other. The natural and free development of the surroundings of the court gardener's house contrasts with the palace, which is »manifold and yet one« (Friedrich Wilhelm IV). The system of an open and yet simultaneously fixed order of buildings, open spaces, prescribed direction and random movement, the official and private relationships between Crown Prince and court gardener, between court guests and walkers, masters and servants, between the court gardener's domestic economy and the court society have the effect of an idealizing transfiguration of the class system, of newly developed and traditional rules in harmony with eternal progress and constant change.

In the large arbour the staircase is at the heart of the composition that for its part holds together the heterogeneous components of the group of buildings that makes up the Roman Baths. Schinkel had seen and drawn a double-flight staircase like this on his first Italian journey in a farmstead in Anacapri. That drawing must have been the basis for a large number of sketches by Schinkel and Crown Prince when arriving at a form for the Roman Baths. Double-flight staircases are an old motif for climbing out of the darkness into light; thus they are found in Egyptian temples, on pictures of the Tower of Babel, and finally in designs for Heinrich Gentz's and Friedrich Gilly's memorial to Frederick the Great. The staircase in Schinkel's designs for *The Magic Flute* has a parallel significance. In this case it is the place of purification for Tamino and Pamina: at the end of their trial by fire and water it takes the couple up into the light of Sarastro's temple.

The seat under the great lime tree is a Bacchic place. The entablature is supported by two colossal herms of Dionysus, Christian Daniel Rauch's relief behind the marble table shows a bacchanalian scene, flanked by tondi of Pan and satyrs; on the half-high wall are kraters, also decorated with bacchanalian scenes. It is thus a place that invites the wanderer to rest, promising him refreshment by food and drink, in correspondence with the porch in front of the kitchen entrance opposite, and given the abundance of fruit and exquisite vegetables in the Italian Orchard, also

encouraging a lavish banquet. But Schinkel did not allow wanderers to linger here (and not just in the drawing). The whole area under the large arbour symbolizes the way of purification from enjoyment to elevation (Bacchus/Dionysus) and the decision between sensuality and virtue (Hercules). Dionysus and Hercules, who were born to Zeus by mortal mothers, earned the right to Olympus only through this purification and decision. The way begins at the sarcophagus that serves as a fountain trough under the front herm; the trough carries an image of a bearded Dionysus as »provider of wine«. Fish providing water and a shell are a reminder of Dionysus's attachment to the sea and the underworld, and the centaur relief on the sarcophagus reminds us of the battle between the Centaurs and the Lapiths, which was caused by excessive consumption of wine. The second herm, from whose table a fountain also bubbles, bordering the seating area supports a young Dionysus with wings on his headband; he is called »provider of wings«. Below him is set a statuette of Hercules: Hercules at the parting of the ways. Even the diagonal show bed described by Pliny (»demissus inde pronusque pulvinus, cui bestiarum effigies invicem adversas buxus inscripsit«, *Letters*, V, 6, 16) is part of the whole, in that it is intended to be read like a relief from left to right, while walking along its length. The flight of steps invites us to leave the place of comfort and idleness and to climb up to the bright heights of the flat roof over the arcaded hall. It is only from here that the broad view in full sunlight over to the white Schloß Charlottenhof opens up, that guarantee of eternal laws, and also out over the infinity of the mysterious stretch of water, which disappears into the unexplored darkness.

The great path around the Charlottenhof park constantly offers views back inside the ideal landscape. From the windows of the palace and from the terrace this is possible only in predefined directions. Above the great exedra all we see is »a tower in the town of Potsdam in the distance«, and next to it the monopteros above the military orphanage. A free view is available only from here, from the viewing platform above the roof of the arcaded hall. Schinkel's drawing »Perspective ... on the flat roof« for the *Sammlung architektonischer Entwürfe* offers the decision, right to the palace, left over the wild waters and nature. But in the centre it places the fountain jet in the great garden courtyard, behind which the decorated candelabrum with the plume of smoke from the steam engine can be seen, and a votary as the central acroterion on the tea pavilion, seeming to worship the elements of fire and water. But on a lost water-colour by Johann Heinrich Hintze the viewer is turning out of the enclosed landscape of Siam. The eye moves over the water of moat and pool into the distance, to the hills in the glacial valley of the Havel. Above the arbour and bordering vegetation the waters of the river shine out with the Telegrafenberg and the Belvedere on the Brauhausberg in the background; on the far left the towers of the city can be seen, the Garrison Church and the Heiligen-Geist-Kirche framing the orphanage's monopteros. While Carl Daniel Freidank's panorama from the Brauhausberg over river valley and town reveals a glimpse of »Siam«, it is possible to make out the world from the roof of the arcaded hall.

It was not until the Crown Prince's »Siam« was largely complete that Lenné commissioned his pre-

ihm steht eine Herkules-Statuette; Herkules am Scheideweg. Auch das von Plinius beschriebene schräge Schaubeet (»demissus inde pronusque pulvinus, cui bestiarum effigies invicem adversas buxus inscripsit«, *Briefe*, V, 6,16) ist Teil des Ganzen, indem es wie ein Relief von links nach rechts abgelesen und dabei abgeschritten werden soll. Der Treppenzug fordert, den Platz des Behagens und des Müßiggangs hinter sich zu lassen, aufzusteigen zur lichten Höhe des flachen Daches über der Arkadenhalle. Allein von hier öffnet sich der weite Blick ins volle Sonnenlicht hinüber zum weißen Schloß Charlottenhof, dem Garanten der ewigen Gesetze, und über die Unendlichkeit der geheimnisvollen Wasserfläche, die in unerforschtem Dunkel verschwindet.

Vom großen Umgehungsweg des Parkes Charlottenhof werden die Blicke immer wieder ins Innere der idealen Landschaft zurückgeworfen. Aus den Fenstern des Schlosses und von der Terrasse werden sie nur in vorbestimmte Richtungen zugelassen. Über der großen Exedra sieht man lediglich »einen Thurm der Stadt Potsdam in der Ferne«, daneben den Monopteros über dem Militärwaisenhaus. Den freischweifenden Blick gibt es erst von hier, von der Aussichtsplattform über dem Dach der Arkadenhalle. Schinkels Zeichnung »Perspective ... auf dem platten Dache« aufgenommen für die *Sammlung Architektonischer Entwürfe* bietet die Entscheidung an, nach rechts zum Schloß, nach links über das wilde Wasser und die Natur. Aber sie rückt in den Mittelpunkt den Strahl der Fontäne im großen Gartenhof, hinter dem der geschmückte Kandelaber mit der Rauchfahne der Dampfmaschine zu sehen ist und ein Adorant als Mittelakroterion auf dem Teepavillon, der die Elemente Feuer und Wasser anzubeten scheint. Auf einem verschollenen Aquarell von Johann Heinrich Hintze wendet sich dagegen der Betrachter aus der umschlossenen Siam-Landschaft hinaus. Über das Wasser von Graben und Teich geht der Blick bis zu den Hügeln des Urstromtals der Havel. Über dem Laubengang und der begrenzenden Pflanzung leuchtet das Wasser des Flusses auf mit Telegrafenberg und Belvedere auf dem Brauhausberg im Hintergrund; ganz links sieht man die Türme der Stadt, Garnisonkirche und Heiligen-Geist-Kirche, die den Monopteros des Waisenhauses zwischen sich fassen. Während Carl Daniel Freydanks Panorama vom Brauhausberg aus über Flußtal und Stadt einen Blick auf »Siam« freigibt, kann man vom Dach der Arkadenhalle die Welt erkennen.

Erst als das »Siam« des Kronprinzen weitgehend vollendet war, hat Lenné ein Dokument der Gesamtanlage bei seinem bevorzugten Zeichner Gerhard

Koeber in Auftrag gegeben, die farbige Lithographie »Charlottenhof oder Siam 1839«. Wie eine Insel ist der Park Charlottenhof mit seinen Bauten von einer dichten Randpflanzung umgeben und kann nur über die vom Werderschen Weg her übernommene Lindenallee von der Außenwelt erreicht werden, gleichsam über einen Steg; mit einem großen Fahrweg, der als alles umschließende Parabel geführt wird, ist das Gebiet im Nordwesten und im Nordosten an den friderizianischen Garten angeschlossen. Während die weite Innenfläche des Parkes nur von Fußwegen durchzogen wird, drängen sich an seinem südlichen und nördlichen Rand die Bauten mit ihren Anlagen: im Süden die strenge Achse des Schlosses, vom Sonnenaufgang mit dem Maschinenhaus im Osten, über das Paradies des Rosengartens, die wie ein Altan über die Landschaft erhobene Gartenterrasse, das Schloß selbst, den der Kontemplation dienenden Quincunx nach Westen, das Maiblumenstück, den das Ganze spiegelnden Karpfenteich und die Ildefonso-Gruppe dahinter, schließlich im westlichen Waldesdunkel verborgen der Hippodrom; im Osten, am Schafgraben und seiner teichartigen Erweiterung mit den beiden unregelmäßigen Inseln, das Hofgärtnerhaus, der Teepavillon, der überlaubte Kanal und die antiken Räume des Römischen Bades; dazu das westlich vorgelagerte Italienische Kulturstück und die kleinen Schaugärten nach Norden, Orte naturwissenschaftlicher Erfahrung und gärtnerischer Innovation.

Das Dokument der pädagogischen Provinz des Kronprinzen war zugleich Zeugnis von dessen Gefährdung und bevorstehender Zerstörung. Denn als Lenné den Auftrag erteilte, das Ergebnis von seinen und Schinkels Arbeiten festzuhalten, deutete sich bereits an, daß der Kronprinz mit der Plazierung der Fasanerie westlich des Siamgartens die Herausnahme des Hippodroms und damit eine Auflösung der Gesamtanlage und ihrer strengen Konzeption vorsah. Der Hippodrom wurde als Nutzfläche der Fasanenzucht zugeordnet, wobei auf der alten Grundstücksgrenze des zuletzt erworbenen Ackerstücks eine Schneise durch die Waldung geschlagen wurde, die dann den trennenden Zaun zwischen den Bereichen des Hofmarschallamts und des Hofjagdamts aufnahm.

Kurt Kuhlow hat 1907 ein unsigniertes Schreiben Peter Joseph Lenné zugeschrieben: »Zu meiner Freude hörte ich, der Kronprinz werde das neu angelegte Charlottenhof nicht eigentlich bewohnen, den Bezirk einer phantastischen Schöpfung, die Stadt Potsdam im Rücken, so daß das Auge auf der Magie einer fremden, geträumten, ersehnten Welt ruht. Der Thron selbst steht auf einem anderen Boden.«

Ausgewählte Literatur

Börsch-Supan, Helmut, *Karl Friedrich Schinkel. Bühnenentwürfe / Stage Designs*, Berlin 1990.
Büsch, Otto (Hrsg.), *Friedrich Wilhelm IV. in seiner Zeit. Beiträge eines Colloquiums*, Berlin 1987.
Durand, Jean-Nicolas-Louis, *Recueil et parallèle des édifices de tout genre ... dessinés sur une même échelle*, Paris 1799–1801.
Günther, Harri, und Sibylle Harksen, *Peter Joseph Lenné. Katalog der Zeichnungen*, Tübingen und Berlin 1993.
Häberlin-Belani, Carl Ludwig, *Sanssouci, Potsdam und Umgebung*, Berlin und Potsdam 1855.
Hoffmann, Hans, und Renate Möller, *Schloß Charlottenhof und die Römischen Bäder*, Potsdam-Sanssouci 1985.
Ibbeken, Hillert, und Elke Blauert (Hrsg.), *Karl Friedrich Schinkel. Das architektonische Werk heute / The architectural work today*, Stuttgart und London 2002.
Kleist, Heinrich von, über den *Mönch am Meer von Caspar David Friedrich, Berliner Abendblätter*, 13. Oktober 1810.
Kroll, Frank-Lothar, *Friedrich Wilhelm IV. und das Staatsdenken der deutschen Romantik*, Berlin 1990.
Kuhlow, Kurt, »Das Büringsche Vorwerk«, in: *Mitteilungen des Vereins für die Geschichte Potsdams*, NF 5, Heft 6, Nr. 310, 1911.
Kuhlow, Kurt, *Das Königliche Schloß Charlottenhof bei Potsdam*, Berlin 1912.
Peik, Susan M. (Hrsg.), *Karl Friedrich Schinkel. Aspects of his Work / Aspekte seines Werks*, Stuttgart und London 2001.
Percier, Charles, und Pierre François Léonard Fontaine, *Choix des plus célèbres maisons de plaisance de Rome et de ses environs ...*, Paris 1809.
Pundt, Hermann G., *Schinkels Berlin*, Frankfurt am Main, Berlin und Wien 1981.
Schärf, Hartmann Manfred, *Die klassizistischen Landschloßumbauten Karl Friedrich Schinkels*, Berlin 1986.
Karl Friedrich Schinkel. Lebenswerk, hrsg. von Paul Ortwin Rave, seit 1968 von Margarete Kühn, Berlin seit 1939, München und Berlin seit 1968.
Karl Friedrich Schinkel 1781–1841, Berlin 1980.
Schinkel in Potsdam, Potsdam-Sanssouci 1981.
Zadow, Mario Alexander, *Karl Friedrich Schinkel. Ein Sohn der Spätaufklärung*, Stuttgart und London 2001.
Zadow, Mario Alexander, *Karl Friedrich Schinkel. Leben und Werk*, Stuttgart und London 2003.
Zukowsky, John (Hrsg.), *Karl Friedrich Schinkel: The Drama of Architecture*, Chicago, Tübingen und Berlin 1994.

11. Johann Heinrich Hintze, Blick von der Arkadenhalle der Römischen Bäder zur Stadt Potsdam und
zum Brauhausberg, um 1845. Aquarell. Verschollen.
12. Peter Joseph Lenné, *Plan von Charlottenhof oder
Siam*, gezeichnet von Gerhard Koeber, 1839, Farb-
lithographie. SPSG, Planslg. 12152.

11. Johann Heinrich Hintze, view from the arcaded hall
of the Roman Baths towards the city of Potsdam and
the Brauhausberg, c. 1845. Water colour. Missing.
12. Peter Joseph Lenné, *Plan of Charlottenhof or Siam*,
drawn by Gerhard Koeber, 1839, coloured lithograph.
SPSG, Planslg. 12152.

Selected bibliography

Börsch-Supan, Helmut, *Karl Friedrich Schinkel. Bühnen-
entwürfe / Stage Designs*, Berlin, 1990.
Büsch, Otto (ed.), *Friedrich Wilhelm IV. in seiner Zeit.
Beiträge eines Colloquiums*, Berlin, 1987.
Durand, Jean-Nicolas-Louis, *Recueil et parallèle des
édifices de tout genre ... dessinés sur une même
échelle*, Paris, 1799–1801.
Günther, Harri, and Sibylle Harksen, *Peter Joseph
Lenné. Katalog der Zeichnungen*, Tübingen and Berlin,
1993.
Häberlin-Belani, Carl Ludwig, *Sanssouci, Potsdam und
Umgebung*, Berlin and Potsdam, 1855.
Hoffmann, Hans, and Renate Möller, *Schloß Charlotten-
hof und die Römischen Bäder*, Potsdam-Sanssouci,
1985.
Ibbeken, Hillert, and Elke Blauert (eds.), *Karl Friedrich
Schinkel. Das architektonische Werk heute / The archi-
tectural work today*, Stuttgart and London, 2002.
Kleist, Heinrich von, on the *Mönch am Meer* by Cas-
par David Friedrich, *Berliner Abendblätter*, 13 October
1810.
Kroll, Frank-Lothar, *Friedrich Wilhelm IV. und das Staats-
denken der deutschen Romantik*, Berlin, 1990.
Kuhlow, Kurt, »Das Büringsche Vorwerk«, in: *Mitteilun-
gen des Vereins für die Geschichte Potsdams*, NF 5,
Heft 6, Nr. 310, 1911.
Kuhlow, Kurt, *Das Königliche Schloß Charlottenhof bei
Potsdam*, Berlin, 1912.
Peik, Susan M. (ed.), *Karl Friedrich Schinkel. Aspects of
his Work / Aspekte seines Werks*, Stuttgart and London,
2001.
Percier, Charles, und Pierre François Léonard Fontaine,
*Choix des plus célèbres maisons de plaisance de Rome
et de ses environs ...*, Paris, 1809.
Pundt, Hermann G., *Schinkel's Berlin*, Cambridge, Mass.,
1972.
Schärf, Hartmann Manfred, *Die klassizistischen Land-
schloßumbauten Karl Friedrich Schinkels*, Berlin, 1986.
Karl Friedrich Schinkel. Lebenswerk, edited by Paul Ort-
win Rave, since 1968 by Margarete Kühn, Berlin, since
1939, München and Berlin, since 1968.
Karl Friedrich Schinkel 1781–1841, Berlin, 1980.
Schinkel in Potsdam, Potsdam-Sanssouci, 1981.
Zadow, Mario Alexander, *Karl Friedrich Schinkel. Ein
Sohn der Spätaufklärung*, Stuttgart and London, 2001.
Zadow, Mario Alexander, *Karl Friedrich Schinkel. Leben
und Werk*, Stuttgart and London, 2003.
Zukowsky, John (ed.), *Karl Friedrich Schinkel: The Drama
of Architecture*, Chicago, Tübingen and Berlin, 1994.

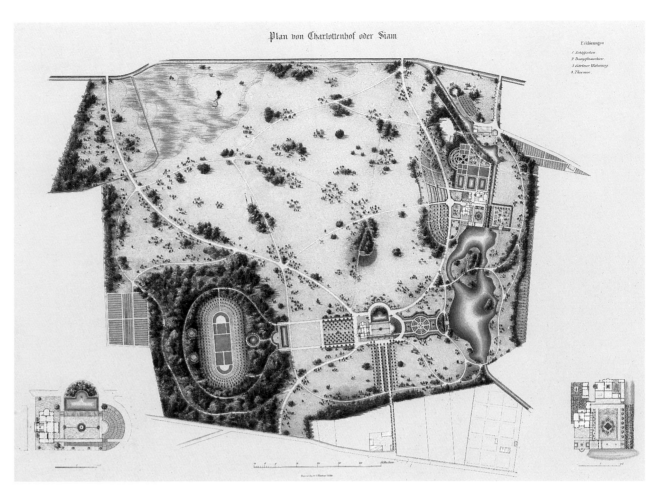

ferred draughtsman, Gerhard Koeber, to document
the complex as a whole, which resulted in the colour
lithograph »Charlottenhof oder Siam 1839«. The Charlottenhof park and its buildings are surrounded like an
island by the dense peripheral planting. It can only be
approached from the outside world by the avenue of
limes taken over from the Werderscher Weg, almost
as if by bridge; a large carriage drive, running as an
all-embracing parabola, links the site to Frederick the
Great's garden in the north-east and north-west. While
only footpaths run through the extensive interior of
the park, the buildings and their surrounding features
crowd at the southern and northern edge: in the south
is the austere axis of the Palace, starting at sunrise
with the engine house in the north-east, via the Garden of Eden of the Rose Garden, the garden terrace,
raised above the landscape like a balcony, the Palace
itself, the quincunx, for contemplation, to the west,
the mayflower area, the carp pool, reflecting the whole
with the Ildefonso group beyond it, and finally, hidden
in the dark of the western woods, the Hippodrome; in
the east, by the Schafgraben and its pool-like extension with the two irregular islands, the court gardener's
house, the tea pavilion, the canal with its arch of foliage and the ancient rooms of the Roman Baths; in addition to this there is the area of the Italian Orchard in
front on the western side and the small show gardens
to the north, places for scientific experiment and horticultural innovation.

The document of the Crown Prince's pedagogic
province was at the same time evidence of the threat
to it and its eventual destruction. For as Lenné issued
the commission to record the outcome of his and
Schinkel's work, there were already signs that the
Crown Prince, by placing the pheasantry west of the

Siam garden was intending to remove the Hippodrome and thus break up the complex as a whole,
along with the rigid concept behind it. The Hippodrome was allotted to the pheasantry as a breeding
ground, and an aisle was cut through the wood on the
old site boundary of the most recently acquired piece
of arable land; this then accommodated the fence
that divided the areas between the major-domo's office and the court hunting office.

In 1907 Kurt Kuhlow attributed an unsigned letter
to Peter Joseph Lenné: »To my delight I heard that the
Crown Prince is not actually intending to live in the
newly landscaped Charlottenhof, the area of a fantas-
tic creation, with the city of Potsdam at its back, so
that the eye comes to rest on the magic of a strange,
dreamed, longed-for world. The throne itself stands
on other ground.«

1. Im Anflug auf das Schloß Charlottenhof von Westen erkennt man die klare Achse des Schlosses und nordöstlich davon im Gegensatz dazu die lockere Baugruppe der Römischen Bäder.
2. Das Flugbild von Norden her zeigt die Anordnung des Schlosses mit Terrasse, Exedra und den weiten konzentrischen Kreisen des Rosengartens nach Osten hin.
3. Die Römischen Bäder präsentieren sich im Anflug von Norden als lockere Baugruppe in dennoch starker Bindung mit Beziehung zum Maschinenteich und seiner natürlich geformten Insel.

1. Approaching Schloß Charlottenhof from the west in a plane the clear axis of the Palace can be made out, and north-east of this, the contrasting, loose group of buildings making up the Roman baths.
2. The aerial photograph from the north shows how the Palace is arranged with terrace, exedra and the broad concentric circles of the Rose Garden to the east.
3. The Roman Baths seen from the air from the north appear as loosely-grouped buildings, but strongly connected with the machine pool and its naturally formed island.

4–6. Die Gartenfassade von Schloß Charlottenhof erhebt sich strahlend über der künstlichen Terrasse und spiegelt sich in dem vorgelagerten Wasserbecken. Die nach über 100 Jahren zu einem majestätischen Baum herangewachsene Platane setzt wie die Säule mit dem Bildnis der Hausherrin, Kronprinzessin Elisabeth, Maßstäbe für die umgebende Landschaft mit dem nach Westen abschließendem dunklen Waldessaum.

4–6. The garden façade of Schloß Charlottenhof rises radiantly over the artificial terrace and is reflected in the pools of water in front of it. The plane tree, which after over 100 years has grown to a majestic height, together with the column with the portrait of the lady of the house, Crown Princess Elisabeth, sets the scale for the surrounding landscape with the dark fringe of woodland that forms its western conclusion.

7–9. Seine strengste Ansicht hat das Schloß nach Norden. Der klar vorspringende Halbzylinder betont das harte Rechteck des Hauptgeschosses über dem niedrigen angeböschten Souterrain. Auch die Westseite des Schlosses gibt sich streng und verschlossen, allein durchbrochen von dem hohen Portikus, der mit seinem ägyptisierenden Portal wie eine Tempelfront wirkt. Dieser Portikus ist weniger ein Eingang als ein Platz zum Verweilen vor dem Haus, der wie der entsprechende Platz am Kasino von Glienicke als ein Sitzplatz für Vorübergehende, Wartende, Kontemplierende ausgebildet ist.

7–9. The most austere view from the Palace is to the north. The clearly protruding half-cylinder emphasizes the hard rectangle of the main floor on the low banked-up basement. The western side of the Palace also presents an austere and closed front, broken only by the high portico which, together with its Egyptian-style portal, seems like a temple façade. This portico is less an entrance than a place in which to linger outside the building, arranged, in the same way as the corresponding place in the Glienicke casino as a place to sit for passers-by, people waiting and those of a contemplative nature.

10, 11. Das Vestibül öffnet sich dem von Westen Eintretenden in abendlicher Kühle. Mit dem Oberlicht aus dunkelblauem Glas und goldenen Sternen zitiert Schinkel die Sternenhalle der Königin der Nacht aus seiner Dekoration zur *Zauberflöte*.

10, 11. The vestibule offers the cool of the evening to visitors entering from the west. Schinkel's skylight with dark-blue glass and golden stars is a quotation from the Queen of the Night's starry hall in his stage designs for *The Magic Flute*.

12–15. Mit dem nüchtern ausgestatteten Vorzimmer öffnet sich die Wohnung des Kronprinzenpaares. Das graphikgeschmückte Kabinett des Hausherrn leitet über zum gemeinsamen Schlafraum hinter dem Halbzylinder der Nordfassade, aus dem drei Fenster drei verschiedene Blicke auf Morgen-, Mittag- und Abendlandschaft richten – so wie auf die drei unterschiedlichen Meere aus der Villa des Plinius. Pfeilerhohe Spiegel führen zwischen den Fensterausblicken den Raum weiter in die Tiefe der Landschaft.

12–15. The Crown Prince's and Crown Princess's apartments open with the austerely furnished anteroom. The Prince's small private chamber, decorated with graphic art, forms a transition to the joint bedroom behind the half-cylinder of the north façade, from which three windows provide three different views of the morning, midday and evening landscape – just as Pliny's villa overlooked three different seas. Pier glasses between the views out of the windows take the room deeper into the depths of the landscape.

16–18. Kostbarster Raum der kronprinzlichen Wohnung ist das Kabinett der Hausherrin in Rosé, Meergrün und Silber mit dem von Schinkel gestalteten Schreibplatz und den wunderbaren silbernen Türen. Von hier aus geht der Blick zurück durch das Schlafzimmer zum einfachen Kabinett des Hausherrn.

16–18. The most luxurious room in the Crown Prince's apartments is the Crown Princess's small chamber in pink, sea-green and silver with its writing area designed by Schinkel and the wonderful silver doors. From here the view is back through the bedroom to the Prince's simple private chamber.

19–22. Aus dem Wohnzimmer geht es durch den Gartensaal mit den Statuen von Ganimed und David in ein Kupferstichzimmer, das vielfältigen Zwecken dienen kann.

19–22. The living-room leads through the garden-room with statues of David and Ganymede into a small gallery for engravings that can serve various purposes.

23, 24. Auf der anderen Seite des Hauses erlauben die Zwecke der Räume eine größere Ungebundenheit. Ein Eckkabinett markiert mit Fenster- und Türausblicken und den kolorierten Landschaftsradierungen Bleulers den Übergang zwischen Norden und Süden und leitet über in das Zeltzimmer der schweifenden Phantasie.
25–28. Schinkels strenger antikisierender Schreibsekretär öffnet sich zu gotischer Intimität und offenbart mit einer Vielzahl unterschiedlichster Behältnisse seine Multifunktionalität.

23, 24. On the other side of the building the purpose of the rooms is less defined. A small corner room with views through windows and doors mark and Bleuler's coloured landscape etchings marks the transition from north to south and leads through into the tented room of soaring fantasy.
25–28. Schinkel's austere bureau in the ancient style opens up into Gothic intimacy and reveals its many functions with a large variety of containers.

29. Der Gartenportikus mit seinen strengen dorischen Säulen stellt die Bühne dar, auf der die Bewohner des Hauses der Welt des umgebenden Gartens gegenübertreten.
30, 31. Die Gartenterrasse erstreckt sich zwischen Gartenportikus und großer Exedra. Sie ist zugleich Bühne und Zuschauerraum.

29. The garden portico with its austere Doric columns represents the stage on which the residents of the building confront the world of the surrounding garden.
30, 31. The garden terrace runs between the garden portico and the great exedra. It is a stage and auditorium in one.

32, 33. Die große Exedra lädt ein zum Sitzen auf den Gräbern der Vorfahren, einer unverputzten Mauer mit eingelassenen Grabnischen.

32, 33. The large exedra presents an invitation to sit on ancestors' graves, an unrendered wall with tomb niches let into it.

34, 35. Die Todessymbolik der Mauer mit den Urnennischen zu überwinden, bietet sich eine Treppe zwischen Apoll und Clio an, die steil auf die Höhe der Pergola auf der Südseite der Gartenterrasse führt.

34, 35. In order to overcome the death symbolism of the wall with its urn niches there is the possibility of using a staircase between Apollo and Clio leading steeply to the level of the pergola on the south side of the garden terrace.

36. Von der Gartenterrasse geht der Blick über die bewegte Landschaft zu den Römischen Bädern.
37. Westansicht der Römischen Bäder. Von links nach rechts: Gehilfenwohnung, Hofgärtnerwohnung, Teepavillon des Kronprinzen.
38. Westansicht der Hofgärtnerwohnung.

36. From the garden terrace the eye is led over the lively landscape to the Roman Baths.
37. View of the Roman Baths from the west. From left to right: staff accommodation, court gardener's accommodation, Crown Prince's tea pavilion.
38. View of the court gardener's accommodation from the west.

51

39–41. Man betritt den Bereich des Hofgärtners durch eine große Laube, die einen bacchantischen Sitzplatz überfängt. Der Kronprinz als Hausherr ist in Gestalt seines Necknamens als gewaltiger Butt anwesend und speiht wie eine Lebensquelle das Wasser über die große Muschel in den Kentaurensarkophag.

39–41. The court gardener's realm is entered through a large arbour enclosing a bacchanalian seating area. The Crown Prince is present as the owner of the house in the form of his nickname as an enormous flounder, spewing water like a life-giving spring over the great shell in the centaur's sarcophagus.

S. 54, 55
42, 43. Die Pergola an der Ostseite des Hofgärtnerhauses leitet den Blick in die Tiefe durch den Teepavillon auf die Wasserfläche des Maschinenteichs
und umgekehrt in die Höhe zu einer schmalen, ins
Licht führenden Treppe zur Aussichtsplattform über
der Arkadenhalle.

pp. 54, 55
42, 43. The pergola on the east side of the court gardener's house down through the tea pavilion to the surface of the water of the machine pool and conversely
upwards to a narrow staircase leading into the light of
the viewing platform above the arcaded hall.

44–46. Der in seinem Äußeren als Tempel ausgebildete Teepavillon enthüllt sich in seinem Inneren als lichtdurchfluteter Raum mit den unterschiedlichsten Ausblicken zum überlaubten Kanal, auf die Gartenterrasse mit ihrem ornamentierten Pflaster, in den Garten und auf die Wasserfläche des Maschinenteichs. Das Mittelsofa, dessen Schaft Amazonen mit ihren männlichen Gefangenen darstellt, trägt im Polster die Lieblingsblumen der Königin Luise, Rosen und Kornblumen.

44–46. The tea pavilion, whose exterior in the form of a temple is a light-flooded room inside, with a variety of views over the canal with its arbour of foliage, of the garden terrace with its ornamental paving, and of the surface of the machine pool. The central sofa, whose shaft represents Amazons with their male captives, has Queen Luise's favourite flowers, roses and cornflowers, on its upholstery.

47, 48. An der Rückseite des Teepavillons und mit Blick auf die rosenbewachsene Südseite des Hofgärtnerhauses stehen unter tempelartigen Baldachinen die Büsten der Eltern des Kronprinzen mit einer Brunnenschale zwischen ihnen.

47, 48. Busts of the Crown Prince's parents with a fountain bowl between them stand under temple-like baldachinos at the rear of the tea pavilion, with a view of the south side of the court gardener's house, which is covered with roses.

49–51. Von den Dächern über der Arkadenhalle und den pompejanischen Räumen geht der Blick weit über die Gartenlandschaft und zum Schloß Charlottenhof; ehemals soll man von hier die Türme der Stadt Potsdam und stückweise den blinkenden Flußlauf der Havel gesehen haben.

49–51. From the roofs over the arcaded hall and the Pompeian rooms the eye is taken far over the garden landscape to Schloß Charlottenhof; formerly it is said to have been possible to see the towers of the town of Potsdam from here, and parts of the sparkling course of the River Havel.

52–54. Der erste Bauabschnitt der römischen Zimmer war die Arkadenhalle. Hier wird deutlich, daß die scheinbar zwanglose Anordnung des Bauensembles geheime axiale Bindungen hat. Aus dem Impluvium durch das Atrium über die Fontäne des großen Gartens zur Säule des Germanicus ergibt sich eine strenge Richtung.

52–54. The first building phase of the Roman rooms was the arcaded hall. Here it is clear that the seemingly informal arrangement of the building ensemble has secret axial links. A strong line leads out of the impluvium through the atrium via the fountain in the great garden to the column of Germanicus.

55–57. Ausgrabungen in Pompeji waren der Anlaß für die Baderäume hinter der Arkadenhalle. Im Vestibül begrüßen Dionysos und Apoll den Eintretenden. Dahinter liegt ein Impluvium mit wirklich offenem Dach, dann folgen ein Salbraum und zur Linken die eigentlichen Thermen, vor derem tiefergelegenen Becken vier Koren Wache halten.

55–57. Excavations in Pompeii prompted the baths behind the arcaded hall. Dionysus and Apollo greet visitors in the vestibule. Beyond this is an impluvium with a genuinely open roof, then an ointment room and on the left the actual thermal baths, with four caryatids standing guard in front of the sunken pool.

58, 59. Hinter den Koren erfüllt eine Dachöffnung das Badebecken mit vollem Licht. Auch der konzentrierte, in sich abgeschiedene Raum des Billardzimmers erhält sein Licht durch eine Öffnung im Dach.

58, 59. An opening in the roof behind the caryatids floods the bathing pool with light. The compact and isolated billiard room is also lit from an opening in the roof.